ECONOMIC AND
SOCIAL INVESTIGATIONS IN
MANCHESTER, 1833—1933

ECONOMIC AND
SOCIAL INVESTIGATIONS IN
MANCHESTER, 1833–1933

A Centenary History of the
Manchester Statistical Society

BY

T. S. ASHTON

READER IN CURRENCY AND PUBLIC FINANCE IN
THE UNIVERSITY OF MANCHESTER

With an Introduction by the Rt. Hon.

THE EARL OF CRAWFORD AND BALCARRES

K.T., P.C., F.R.S.

and an

INDEX OF REPORTS AND
PAPERS OF THE SOCIETY

AUGUSTUS M. KELLEY • PUBLISHERS
FAIRFIELD 1977

Published in the U.S.A. 1977 by
AUGUSTUS M. KELLEY, Publishers
Fairfield, New Jersey 07006, USA

*Economic and Social Investigations
in Manchester, 1833–1933*
first published in 1934 by
P. S. King & Son Ltd, London

This reprint first published in 1977
by The Harvester Press Limited
Hassocks, Sussex, England

Library of Congress Cataloging in Publication Data

Ashton, Thomas Southcliffe.
  Economic and social investigations in Manchester,
  1833–1933.
  Reprint of the 1934 ed. published by P. S. King,
  London.
  Includes index.
  1. Manchester Statistical Society, Manchester,
  Eng. 2. Social surveys—England—Manchester.
  3. Great Britain—Social conditions. I. Title.
  HA1.M33A73 1977 310'.6'242733 77–3570

  ISBN 0–678–08067–4

Printed and manufactured in Great Britain

PREFACE

THE preparation of this brief History has involved much close reading of Reports and Transactions. This has brought a reward that is quite inadequately reflected in the following pages. The men who made our Society also made much of what is best in the traditions and culture of Manchester. To share their thoughts and to understand their aspirations, is to enlarge one's own life.

The task of making the book has been lightened by much generous help. Dr. James Bonar, Mr. H. W. Macrosty, and Professor Hermberg of Jena, have supplied several references. Mr. J. Broatch, Hon. Editor of the Transactions, made a search through the files of the *Manchester Guardian* of the forties and early fifties. Mr. A. H. Allman, Hon. Secretary of the Society, has assisted in innumerable ways; and, throughout, the author has had the advice of a past President, Professor G. W. Daniels. The deepest debt of gratitude is, however, due to another past President, Mr. Barnard Ellinger, not only for the labour he has given in compiling the index of papers and authors, but also for constant stimulus and friendly criticism.

To the Committee of the College of Technology, to the Directors of Williams Deacon's Bank, and to Mr. H. P. Greg, the author is indebted for permission to reproduce the portraits of Benjamin Heywood, William Langton, and William Rathbone Greg. These illustrations are from photographs, kindly made from the originals, by Mr. C. E. Kerr, of the Department of Photography in the College of Technology. That of

v

Benjamin Heywood was taken in circumstances of extreme difficulty, and the result is a tribute to Mr. Kerr's craftsmanship. Lord Shuttleworth, who has shown much interest in the preparation of the book, supplied the photograph of his father, Sir James Kay-Shuttleworth.

T. S. ASHTON.

February, 1934.

INTRODUCTION

A HUNDRED years of statistical enterprise—Mr. Ashton tells the story of Manchester's achievement with humour and understanding. Manchester ranks as pioneer in this form of organised research, though at an earlier period England had already cultivated the statistical mind. For instance, we were in the forefront of compiling vital statistics, such as the Bills of Mortality of the sixteen-sixties, while Sir William Petty was among the first of our political economists to base an argument upon statistical research. But the science of tabulating accurate numbers, values and measurements fell into disrepute. By the end of the eighteenth century our methods were lax and their results misleading. Our system of medical statistics had scarcely changed since the time of James I, and early census returns were full of absurdities. Arthur Young's estimate of the size of England and Wales was several million acres wrong—and, incidentally, Mr. Pitt based estimates for Income Tax yields upon these faulty computations. The Army Authorities had published health returns from 1817 onwards, which can still be studied with profit; military tradition in statistics is robust, for one may suppose that the primitive and primeval statistical feat was that of the tribal Chief, who guessed the number of recruits by counting the adult male population : his second effort would, no doubt, be to use the information for imposing a poll tax. But England grew apathetic— here is a lament of 1835 about our indifference to these things : " What with nonsense verses, novel reading, Apocrypha controversies, and Phrenology afterwards, we have no time to attend to such matters."

The Society of which I have the honour to be President was formed in September 1833. Mr. Ashton's chapter "Early Social Surveys," indicates our prevailing attitude at a moment when national prosperity was clouded by economic disturbance and accompanied by the disclosure of social conditions which were terrifying. Thoughtful men asked themselves how and why these things had been overlooked, how long the squalor and disease had been accumulating. The early records of the Society illustrate the deep-seated alarm, but also the technical interest and curiosity, aroused by the compilation and measurement of relevant facts, which gave a sense of growing mastery of the statistical situation. I fancy that the Society wisely (and perhaps almost unconsciously at the outset) chose the correct method of conducting its affairs.

A Statistical Society differs from an economic or political or social group of inquirers, in that its business (as indeed our own fundamental rule directs) can perfectly well exclude party politics. Figures about housing or diet or education may be comparative or descriptive, but the statistician as such must begin by living in the past. He must in the first place deal with the tendencies elicited by the facts before he can handle the causes or canvass the remedy. A statistical thesis should therefore rest upon the cool and unemotional foundation of science: hence its authority. Thus, the Manchester Society of a century ago could conduct inquiries which no Government could then have undertaken without exciting the distrust inspired by an inquisition, or the suspicion aroused by a tax collector. Let me add that the increasing complexity of current statistical research, and the growing accuracy of system arising from more precise definition and more exact methods of presentation, are giving rise to a new danger—namely, that of congestion. I recently studied a report prepared by well-qualified inquirers into a succinct problem connected with a centralised and well-defined industry. The main facts were duly set forth, but honesty of purpose, the impulse to complete every aspect of the picture, and the reluctance to overlook any possible margin of error, added one qualification after another. The whole issue was so much confused and obfuscated that the plain man was bewildered and could not gather if the unanimous intention was friendly or critical. Anyhow, both interpretations have been placed upon the report.

It was not this over-elaboration which brought about the attack on statistics forty years ago, when *The Quarterly Review* thought it necessary to publish twenty pages on " The Abuse of Statistics "; the criticism was rather directed against the " cheap fancy and sentimentalism " which were said to invade the field of figures. The Manchester Society seems to have held the balance very fairly. It is creditable that our area should have avoided particularisation in respect of the textile industries, and to have evenly divided our effort between social and commercial research. The subordinate verities have throughout been handled with due regard to their relation with the great factors of humanity; activities have always been directed towards constructive and public-spirited objectives—*Beatus qui intelligit.* . . .

I feel confident that our most recent development— namely, the foundation of study groups—will prove beneficial. Their proceedings will be less formal than the regular meetings of the Society. They will provide excellent opportunities for discussing current problems of statistical method and practice, at short notice if necessary, and without the more serious apparatus of the written essay and set debate. I commend the study groups to the rising generation of Lancashire men, for every trade and industry and calling in our county is vitally concerned with our statistical effort. Those who carry centenary burdens upon their shoulders hope that the development of statistical study will be actively pursued by younger students, for the importance of accurate, well-tested, and well-presented data, is more than ever acknowledged.

CRAWFORD AND BALCARRES.

CONTENTS

CHAP.   PAGE

I. THE FOUNDERS 1

II. EARLY SOCIAL SURVEYS 13

III. MORTALITY TABLES AND RAILWAY LABOUR . . . 34

IV. THE PUBLIC HEALTH CONTROVERSY 45

V. THE STRUGGLE FOR PUBLIC EDUCATION 59

VI. INDUSTRIAL FLUCTUATIONS AND BANKING POLICY . . 69

VII. THE WORK OF STANLEY JEVONS AND OTHERS . . . 87

VIII. SOCIAL CURRENTS, 1870–1900 99

IX. THE COTTON INDUSTRY AND POPULATION STATISTICS . . 108

X. THE TWENTIETH CENTURY 117

XI. DOMESTIC AFFAIRS 125

APPENDIX A 138

APPENDIX B 140

APPENDIX C 141

CHAPTER I

THE FOUNDERS

THE Statistical Society of Manchester came into being
at a point of time momentous in the development of
Manchester life. Between 1821 and 1831 the population of the town had increased by no less than 45 per
cent.—a rate of growth probably never before, and
certainly never since, equalled.[1] After the post-war
depression, with its social upheaval and political unrest,
the pace of industrial progress had quickened vastly;
and in 1830 new opportunities of expansion had been
afforded by the opening of the Liverpool and Manchester
Railway. Politically, moreover, Manchester was beginning to count; for though five years were yet to
pass before its incorporation, and twenty before its eleva-
tion to the rank of city, the importance of the town had
just been recognised by the grant of two seats in the
reformed Parliament of 1833.

Nor were these signs of material advance without
their counterpart in the field of intellectual achievement.
From 1515 Manchester had had her Grammar School,
" set up for the promotion of Godliness and good learn-
ing." She could justly boast of possessing in Chetham's
Hospital (founded in 1651) the oldest Blue-Coat School,
and the oldest free library in the country. Her Literary
and Philosophical Society, established in 1781 by Thomas
Percival and his friends, had become famous for its
association with that greatest of Manchester's long line
of scientists, John Dalton; and the union of scholarship
and social idealism that was to give birth to the Statistical

---

[1] Excluding that of Salford, the population of Manchester in 1821
was 129,035 and in 1831, 187,022.

Society had already borne fruit in the Manchester Board of Health, established by Percival in 1796. The war with the French had called a halt in such developments, but after 1815 the growth of institutions was rapid. Between 1821 and 1831 no fewer than four weekly newspapers, including the *Manchester Guardian*, were established in the town. And the spirit of inquiry of the place and time was reflected in such bodies as the Natural History Society (1821), which laid the foundations of the Museum; the Royal Manchester Institution (1823), forerunner of the Art Galleries; the Mechanics' Institution (1824), out of which has grown the College of Technology; and the Royal Medical College (1824), from which has sprung the Medical School of the University. Clearly the reading of local history that leaves the impression of a crude agglomeration of eager manufacturers and brutalised workers is incomplete. Whatever might be true of other urban products of the Industrial Revolution, Manchester a hundred years ago was something more than " the barracks of an industry."

Yet things were far from well. The rapid natural increase of population was intensified by the influx of migrants from the rural areas and from across the Irish Sea. No town could build quickly enough to provide proper homes for the newcomers. They crowded into the houses that the middle class vacated as they moved to the green fields and purer air of the outskirts. They packed into cellar dwellings along the banks of the Irwell and Medlock—open sewers that bore to the sea the refuse of many towns on a stream so slow that the sparrows could find footing on the filth that encrusted its surface. Their standards of living, their habits and creeds, seemed to offer a menace to the native culture of Manchester; and their presence placed undue strain on the yet tender organs of municipal control.

Corporate maladies on a scale hitherto unknown made it imperative that Manchester men should turn to social inquiry. Scientific development provided the instrument. The period saw the beginning of a new type of

Economics, realistic and inductive, based on what had formerly been known as political or social arithmetic. "It is indeed truly said," wrote the Council of the Statistical Society of London [1] in 1838, "that the spirit of the present age has an evident tendency to confront the figures of speech with the figures of arithmetic; it being impossible not to observe a growing distrust of mere hypothetical theory and *a priori* assumption, and the appearance of a general conviction that, in the business of social science, principles are valid for application only inasmuch as they are legitimate induction from facts, accurately observed and methodically classified. . . ." Institutions of various kinds sprang up to develop the new study. In 1832 Lord Auckland and C. E. Poulett Thomson, M.P. for Manchester, established at the Board of Trade a Statistical Office. In the following year, at the meeting of the British Association in Cambridge, a Statistical Section was brought into being. And the demand for quantitative data was registered during the thirties, not only in the growing output of official blue-books, but also in the appearance of such works as McCulloch's *Dictionary of Commerce* (1832), and *Statistical Account of the British Empire* (1837), Porter's *Progress of the Nation* (1836–43), and Marshall's *Digest* (1833), of which three thousand copies were purchased by the Government and distributed to members of the reformed Parliament.

Such were the forces, social and intellectual, that produced the Manchester Statistical Society. It came into being in the autumn of 1833, just after the meeting of the British Association, and some months before the birth of the London Society, now known as the Royal Statistical Society. It was thus the first of its kind in this country, though abroad the Statistical Society of Saxony [2] had been formed in Dresden as early as 1830;

[1] *Journal of the Statistical Society of London*, Vol. I., p. 8.
[2] *Ibid.*, No. 1, p. 110. See also *Das Statistische Büreau für das Königreich Sachsen in den ersten 50 Jahren seines Bestehens* (Leipzig, 1881) and an article by Professor F. Burghardt in *Deutsches Statistisches Zentralblatt*, 23 Jahrgang (1931), p. 193.

and Mexico can perhaps claim that its Society,[1] set up in
the spring of 1833, is the next oldest surviving in the
world to-day.   The Manchester Society was the pattern
on which were modelled the statistical societies of Bristol
(November 1836), Liverpool (January 1838), Ulster
(February 1838), Glasgow (February 1836), Birmingham
(1835), and Leeds (January 1838).   But most of these
had but a brief existence, and to-day Manchester is the
only provincial city with a society of its own.

The founders consisted of a small group of friends, all
under forty years of age, all men of philanthropic and
literary taste, and all connected in some degree with local
industry or banking.   Among them pride of place must
be given to William Langton, for it was in his mind that
the project was conceived, and it is evident from the
records that much of the drudgery that is inseparable
from the life of voluntary associations—and so often
unrecognised—was his.

Born in Yorkshire in 1803, the son of a Preston
merchant, Langton had received his early education in
Switzerland, France, Italy and Germany.   Between 1821
and 1829 he was in business in Liverpool as an agent for
firms in Russia.   Here he came into contact with the
Provident Society, a body of citizens who, under the
influence of Elizabeth Fry, took the responsibility of
visiting the poor with the object of " recommending
sobriety, cleanliness, forethought and method."   In
1829 he came to Manchester to take up the post of
cashier in Heywood's Bank,[2] and in March 1833,
together with others, he set up the Manchester and
Salford District Provident Society " for the encouragement of frugality and forethought, the suppression of
mendicity and imposture and the occasional relief of
sickness and unavoidable misfortune amongst the poor." [3]

[1] The Société Mexicaine de Géographie et Statistique is referred to
in a note in the *Journal of the American Statistical Association* (June, 1933).
[2] As successor to Matthew Nicholson, himself a Liverpool man.   (Leo
Grindon, *Manchester Banks and Bankers*, p. 5.)
[3] H. C. Irvine, *The Old D.P.S.*, p. 5.

It was while secretary to this body that he came to realise the need of some agency for collecting social data, and suggested to his fellow-secretary, Dr. Kay, the desirability of a Statistical Society in the town. Langton was a man of initiative, with a gift for administration. In addition to his work for the Provident Society he was associated with James Heywood in founding the Manchester Athenæum. In 1837 he helped to set up the Manchester Society for Promoting National Education; at a later period he acted as treasurer and secretary to the Chetham Society. In 1846 he was secretary to a committee that aimed at obtaining a University for Manchester; and, though the project did not come to immediate fruition, he is rightly regarded as one of the founders of Owens College, set up in 1851. One of his daughters became the wife of Dr. Greenwood, Principal of the College; and when in 1876 Langton retired from the position of managing director of the Manchester and Salford Bank (which had absorbed Heywood's Bank in 1874) a subscription of £5,000 was raised to create the Fellowship bearing his name at what is now the University of Manchester.

Langton's friend and collaborator, James Phillips Kay, better known as Sir James Kay-Shuttleworth, was born at Rochdale, the son of a cotton manufacturer, in 1804. After serving for a time in the bank of a relative, Mr. Fenton, at Rochdale, he entered the University of Edinburgh at the age of twenty, and in 1827 was admitted to the degree of M.D. In December of that year he took a house in Mosley Street, Manchester, and a few months later was elected Senior Physician to the Ardwick and Ancoats Dispensary.[1] In 1832, when the cholera epidemic raged, he was secretary to the Manchester Board of Health and Physician to the Knott Mill Hospital. It is a remarkable tribute to his energies that at

[1] "Through the dispensary," says Mr. Fay, "the doctor learned at first hand how the poor lived; and in the Parliamentary inquiries of the nineteenth century the evidence of the doctor again and again carried the day." *Great Britain from Adam Smith to the Present Day*, p. 360.

a time when he was engaged in a strenuous battle against the plague, he should have prepared the material for his famous essay on *The Moral and Physical Condition of the Working Classes employed in the Cotton Industry in Manchester*, which called attention to pressing social needs and gave direction to the early inquiries of the Statistical Society.   Dr. Kay's later history belongs to the nation, no less than to Manchester.   In 1835 he was appointed Assistant Poor Law Commissioner in charge of East Anglia.   In 1839, when that forerunner of the Board of Education, the Committee of Council, was set up (largely, it is not too much to claim, as the result of the labours of the Manchester Statistical Society), he became its first secretary.   The following year he established at Battersea the first college for the training of teachers, and in 1849 his services to education were recognised by the conferment of a baronetcy.   To him, more than to any other man, we owe our present system of elementary education. " He was a child of the Industrial Revolution, sturdy, independent-minded, strong-handed and a believer in *labor improbus*.   The foundation of his character was religion.   The instrument of his mental activity was social science.   The decisive factor in his moral judgment was Christian compassion."   So wrote Sir Michael Sadler [1]—and the words are fitting not only of Kay-Shuttleworth, but of each of his colleagues in the early days of the Society.   His association with them lasted only for two years, but his influence was decisive.   In later life he returned to the North ; during the Cotton Famine he acted, under Lord Derby, as Vice-Chairman of the relief committee ; and in 1863 he served as High Sheriff of Lancashire.   He died in May 1877.

Shortly after William Langton's suggestion for the setting up of a statistical society in Manchester, Dr. Kay made a tour in Derbyshire with his friends Samuel and William Rathbone Greg, in the course of which the

---

[1] Frank Smith : *The Life of Sir James Kay-Shuttleworth*. Introduction by Sir Michael Sadler, p. ix.

project took practical shape.[1] These two brothers were the sons of Samuel Greg, the well-known cotton spinner, who had come from Belfast to set up the Quarry Bank Mills at Styal in 1784. The younger Samuel was born in 1804, and was educated at Unitarian Schools in Nottingham and Bristol, and afterwards, for one session, at the University of Edinburgh. In 1832 he took over the Lower House Mill at Bollington, where he built up a model village for more than 300 workpeople and their dependants, and equipped it with playing-fields, a Sunday School, a library and evening classes. His chief energies were devoted for many years to efforts to educate and humanise the workers in his community, and for a time all went well. But in 1846 a strike at the factory brought disappointment and financial loss, and compelled Samuel Greg to retire from business. Though he continued to live in his house near the mill until his death in 1876, it is said that he never had further intercourse with the workpeople whose action, whether justifiable or not, was responsible for so bitter a disillusionment.[2]

The younger brother, William Rathbone Greg, was born in Manchester in 1809, and was also educated at Bristol and Edinburgh. In 1828 he became manager of a mill owned by his father at Bury, and four years later set up in business on his own account in Manchester. But his tastes, like those of his brother, were literary and speculative, rather than financial. He was the author of an essay on *Agriculture and the Corn Laws*, which was awarded a prize of the Anti-Corn Law League ; and apart from his numerous contributions to the Statistical Society, his published works include an essay on *Efforts for the Extinction of the African Slave Trade* (1840),

[1] T. R. Wilkinson, " On the Origin and History of the Manchester Statistical Society," *Transactions*, 1875–6, p. 13.

[2] An account of Samuel Greg is given in the Appendix to a thesis by Miss Frances Collier. He was the author of a volume *Scenes from the Life of Jesus*, and a collection of his papers was published posthumously under the title *A Layman's Legacy*.

The Creed of Christendom (1851), *The Enigmas of Life* (1852), and *Rocks Ahead, or the Warnings of Cassandra* (1874). He was a frequent contributor to the *Edinburgh* and the *Pall Mall*; and it was apparently his literary work—certainly not any faith in tariffs—that earned for him in 1856 the far from onerous post of Commissioner of Customs, and in 1864 that of Comptroller in the Stationery Office. His interest in economic and statistical matters was, no doubt, reinforced by his marriage to the daughter of James Wilson, editor of *The Economist.*

The Gregs, and especially the younger of the two, were indefatigable in the early years of the Society; their intimate knowledge of the cotton industry, their moral enthusiasm and their literary ability did much to point its influence. An older brother, Robert Hyde Greg, became a member in 1834, and, though never in office, he was able to act as a valuable link with other Manchester societies. One of the founders of the Royal Manchester Institution and the Mechanics' Institute, he became President of the Chamber of Commerce, and in 1839, on his return to Parliament as Member for the Borough, he succeeded Poulett Thomson as president of the Anti-Corn Law League.

The conversations of Dr. Kay with the Gregs in Derbyshire resulted in a meeting at the house of Benjamin Heywood, where so many local movements were born and nurtured. In Benjamin Heywood met two of the best strains of northern tradition. For on the paternal side he was descended from Nathaniel Heywood, the nonconforming vicar of Ormskirk and brother of the famous Oliver Heywood; and his mother was the daughter of Dr. Percival, founder of the Literary and Philosophical Society. As early as 1773 his grandfather, Arthur Heywood, had established a bank in Liverpool, and in 1788 his father and uncle had set up the principal banking institution in Manchester, the control of which had now fallen to Benjamin. Born in 1793, he was educated at the University of Glasgow, and at an early age threw himself into the social and political life of Manchester. In 1825, the year after the first Institution was set up by Dr. Birkbeck in London, he brought into being the Manchester Mechanics' Institute, of which he acted as President during its first fifteen years of vigorous life.[1] In 1831 he was returned in the Whig interest as M.P. for Lancashire, and six years later he was created a baronet. His work in initiating exhibitions of art and industry, and the part he played in giving Manchester her first public parks, have been fully described by local historians.[2] His wealth, his social and political influence, and his high personal abilities marked him out for leadership; and, though only thirty-nine years of age, he was some years senior to the other founders of the Society and was naturally elected its first President. In this office he was no mere figure-head. It was his munificence that made possible the early social surveys, and it was relationship with him that largely determined the personnel of the Society. He had married the daughter of a wealthy merchant, Thomas Robinson, and his brother-in-law, Samuel Robinson, a cotton-spinner of Dukinfield (esteemed for his translations from the Persian poets and for his work for public education), was one of the original members of the Society. His intimate connection through his bank with William Langton was cemented by the marriage of two of his sons to two of Langton's daughters. His younger brother James, afterwards Member for North Lancashire, joined the Society during the first session, served as President in 1853–4, and was elected President of the London Statistical Society in 1875. And the tradition was maintained by his son, Oliver, the first freeman of Manchester, who stands, a

[1] Much information about the Manchester Mechanics' Institute and Heywood's part in it is given in the Doctoral thesis of Mabel Phythian-Tylecote : " The Mechanics' Institute Movement in Lancashire and Yorkshire, 1824 to 1850," in the University of Manchester.

[2] See Leo Grindon, *Manchester Banks and Bankers*, p. 185. Benjamin Heywood died at Claremont, Irlams-o'-th'-Height, near Manchester, in 1865.

grave and kindly figure in stone, looking down on the pigeons in Albert Square to-day.

William Langton, James Phillips Kay, Samuel and William Rathbone Greg, Benjamin Heywood—these were our founders. They were men, highly individual but of similar mould, religious but unsentimental, sociable but serious-minded, eager for reform but saved from extremes by fundamental common-sense and a capacity for compromise—the best product of Lancashire genius at a time when Lancashire was beginning to count, not only as a spinner of cotton, but also as a voice in the nation.

Brief mention must be made of the two first Vice-Presidents. Both were Scots whose ancestors lived in Kirkcudbrightshire, and both bore the name of Kennedy, though one of them had it, not by birth, but by adoption on his marriage to an heiress. This was Lieut.-Colonel Shaw-Kennedy (1788–1865), who, after serving gallantly in the Peninsula and at Waterloo, had been made Adjutant-General at Belfast, whence he had been transferred to Manchester in 1827: He was the author of a report on the principles for keeping order during labour disputes, which won the praise of Sir Charles Napier, whose tact and sympathy with the workers have been applauded by more than one recent historian of the Chartist movement. It was probably a kindred interest in the Lancashire operatives that led Shaw-Kennedy to join the Society, which he served as Vice-President in the first session and as President from 1834 to 1836. When, in this last year, he left Manchester to become Inspector-General of the Irish Constabulary in Dublin, he was made a Corresponding Member [1] of the Society, a position he held until his death in 1865.

The career of the other Vice-President, John Kennedy, was very different. Born at Knockmalling in 1769, he

---

[1] Whether from ignorance, or because he was so best remembered in Manchester, successive secretaries printed his name in the list of Corresponding Members with the title of Lieut.-Colonel. Actually he became Major-General in 1845, Lieut.-General in 1854, and General in 1862. The following year he received the K.C.B.

was drawn South by the opportunities of advancement opened up to young Scots by the growing cotton industry of Lancashire. After an apprenticeship of seven years with Cannan and Smith, of Chowbent, he became a partner with James McConnel in the firm of spinners and machine-makers that was to play so important a part in the development of Crompton's mule. He was a friend of Watt, Dalton and Henry; but though of considerable personal attainments, he was a man of modest habits, and continued to live in his house in Ardwick Green to the end of his days. One of his daughters married Samuel Robinson, the brother-in-law of Benjamin Heywood, and another became the wife of Edwin Chadwick, the Poor-Law and sanitary reformer.[1]

It will be evident that few, if any, of the founders of the Society were statisticians in the modern sense of the term. They were less interested in enumeration and computation than in effecting improvement in the state of the people among whom they lived. Like its contemporary the District Provident Society, the Statistical Society was the means to an end. The one stood to the other in the relation of theory to practice, of science to art; and the membership of both bodies is largely identical. Benjamin Heywood was first President of the one and first Treasurer of the other; Shaw-Kennedy was Vice-President, and Langton Secretary of both from the start. And among those who held office in the two societies in their early years were Dr. Kay, Shakespear Phillips, James Heywood, Edward Herford, Henry Romilly, Richard Birley, S. D. Darbyshire, James Aspinall Turner and Henry Houldsworth.

A student with leisure for the task might find it not unprofitable to inquire into the occupations of the early members. He would notice that the cotton industry contributed a strong team, including the Gregs of Styal, James Kennedy of Manchester, Henry and Edmund Ashworth of Bolton, Samuel Robinson of Dukinfield, and

[1] For John Kennedy, see Fairbairn in *Memoirs of the Manchester Literary and Philosophical Society*, 3rd Series, Vol. I; Angus Smith, *ibid.*, Vol. IX; and G. W. Daniels, *The Early English Cotton Industry, passim.*

Thomas Ashton of Hyde (President, 1837–9).   He would
observe the part played by clergymen like the Rev. Edward
Stanley of Alderley (afterwards Bishop of Norwich and
father of Dean Stanley), who served as President in
1836–7; and by nonconformist ministers like the Rev.
J. J. Taylor.   He would discover a long line of medical
men, including John Roberton (President 1844–7),
following in the steps of Dr. Kay.   But most of all he
would be struck by the dominant part played by men
connected with banking.   Whether this was due to the
natural concern of bankers with figures, or to the personal
influence of Benjamin Heywood and William Langton,
it is impossible to say.   Suffice it to register the facts
that the first President and the first Secretary were drawn
from Heywood's Bank, that even the first Treasurer,
Dr. Kay, had served his apprenticeship in Fenton's Bank
at Rochdale, and that original members like Shakespear
Phillips, James Murray, and Henry Newberry, were
founders of the Manchester and Salford Bank in 1836.
When Paul Moon Jones came from the Old Bank in
Birmingham to be managing director of this new institution, one of his first acts was to join the Statistical
Society; and James Macvicar, one of the founders of the
Union Bank, became a member in 1836.

Enough has been said to indicate that the Society had
contact with the life of South-East Lancashire at many
points.   The following pages contain the names of
many men with whom it is the pride of all of us to be
associated.   And even to-day, when there are few so
poorly instructed in the newer economics to do him
reverence, there will be one or two who will recall with
satisfaction the membership of a young man who, though
never in office, attended the meetings and paid his subscription with regularity.   In 1835, and for many years
after, Richard Cobden was of our fellowship.[1]

[1] Cobden was admitted to membership on November 25, 1835.   A
Bank Ledger records the receipt of his subscription of two guineas every
year to 1841; after that date the Ledger gives only the aggregate subscriptions, and it is not possible to say how much longer Cobden retained
his membership.   His name is not in the printed list of members of 1859.

CHAPTER II

EARLY SOCIAL SURVEYS

I

AT its inception the Society consisted, as every successful voluntary association must originally consist, of a body of friends; and the early meetings took place at the home of one or other of the members.[1] When the first of these was held on September 2, 1833, the group, which numbered thirteen, described itself as consisting of " gentlemen accustomed for the most part to meet in private society, and whose habits and opinions are not uncongenial." With a view to uniting the members " by the attractions of an agreeable social intercourse," it was decided that meetings should be held every month, that election should be by strict ballot, and that strangers, not exceeding five in number, might, upon application to the President and Treasurer, be introduced at any meeting. As to its aims, " The Manchester Statistical Society," says the first annual report, " owes its origin to a strong desire felt by its projectors to assist in promoting the progress of social improvement in the manufacturing population by which they are surrounded. Its members are not associated merely for the purpose of collecting facts concerning the condition of the inhabitants of this district, as its name might seem to imply, but the first resolution entered on its minutes pronounces it to be ' a Society for the discussion of subjects of political and social economy, and for the promotion of statistical inquiries, to the total exclusion of party politics.' "

[1] The early meeting-cards state that " the hour and place of meeting will be announced by the Secretaries ten days previously." This continued till at least as late as 1841.

At the second meeting, on October 16, after the rules
had been adopted and the officers elected, the first paper
read before the Society was delivered by W. R. Greg.
It was entitled " A Brief Memoir on the Present State
of Criminal Statistics." On the basis of figures derived
from Spain, France, the Netherlands and Great Britain,
Mr. Greg concluded that " in proportion as education
and its general concomitants, inequality of wealth,
augmented intelligence, increasing commercial and manufacturing activity, and contented population advance in
a province or a county, crimes increase in number and
diminish in atrocity; the more violent give place to
the more mercenary passions; and thefts, frauds and
forgeries prevail instead of murders, highway robberies
and assaults." [1] At the same meeting the members
were presented by Dr. Kay with plans and estimates for
public swimming-baths for the use of the operative
population.[2]

By this time the Society had attracted the attention of
the politicians, and at the third meeting, on November 27,
the "strangers" consisted of five Members of Parliament: the Earl of Kerry (who had much to do with the
founding of the Statistical Society of London), the
Viscount Molyneux, Colonel Evans, G. W. Wood and
Mark Philips. A letter was read from Poulett Thomson, Vice-President of the Board of Trade,[3] who also
sent a volume of official statistics; and the Lord Chancellor, who was anxious to influence the opinions of the
working classes on industrial matters, sent a series of
lectures on Political Economy to Benjamin Heywood,
with the suggestion that members of the Society should
undertake to deliver them at the Mechanics' Institute in
Manchester.[4]

[1] MS. of paper, *Guard Book*, p. 1.
[2] First Report of the Statistical Society, *Guard Book*, p. 9.
[3] Charles Poulett Thomson (1799–1841) had recently been returned,
together with Mark Philips, as representative for Manchester, and sat
for the borough until 1839. In that year he was appointed Governor-
General of Canada and in 1840 was created Baron Sydenham.
[4] The invitation was accepted by several members. Benjamin Hey-

At this meeting Thomas Boothman, jun., presented from the minutes of the Chamber of Commerce a statistical table showing the number of day and Sunday schools in Manchester and Salford, and the number of children in attendance;[1] Samuel Greg read a paper on " The Present State of Education in this and other Countries," and Dr. Kay followed with one on " Defects in the Constitution of Dispensaries," which was subsequently printed.

In this last paper figures were presented of the numbers of patients treated over a series of years at the Royal Infirmary and the dispensaries which, since 1825, had been set up in Chorlton-on-Medlock, Salford and Ardwick.[2] Dr. Kay showed that in 1832 more than one-sixth of the local population had been in receipt of gratuitous medical assistance, and, in language reminiscent of Malthus, generalised " that the reliance of the poor on charitable aid increases as fast as that assistance is provided by the public, and outstrips the natural growth of the population; so that it may be inferred that this loss of independence results in a great degree from the provision made to supply the wants of an infrugal and improvident people." Dr. Kay's remedy was to make the dispensaries largely self-supporting by persuading the workers to subscribe a penny a week each; and, in the spirit of the Poor Law Report of the following year, concluded, " We must make it evident that in the exercise of moral restraint, and by industry, sobriety, a peaceful demeanour, an economical management of their resources, and a far-sighted provision for the day of calamity from which few are exempt, they

---

wood himself opened the series on March 17, 1834, and his lecture was followed by others by Samuel Robinson, G. W. Wood, John Douglass, Dr. Kay, John Cheetham, J. A. Turner, W. R. Wood, E. H. Levyssohn, W. R. Greg, John Davies and William Langton.

[1] 36,770 boys and girls were enrolled at ninety-four Sunday schools, and 3,526 at fourteen day schools, in addition to others at the Grammar School and seven infant schools.

[2] Ardwick and Ancoats Dispensary, January 1829; Hulme, March 28, 1831; Chorlton-on-Medlock, October 13, 1831.

may escape the misery into which imprudent marriages, insobriety, irregularity, turbulence, infrugality and improvidence plunge men gifted by nature with every quality necessary to procure happiness." An Appendix to the paper gives, from Board of Trade tables, the weekly rates of wages paid to different classes of workmen in Manchester, together with a statement of the prices of provisions in the town for each year from 1826 to 1832.

At the fourth meeting, held on January 15, 1834, which was attended by Viscount Morpeth and other guests, Dr. Kay read a report of a conversation that had taken place between Poulett Thomson and members of the Society at Claremont, the home of Benjamin Heywood. Poulett Thomson had announced that there was no prospect of the Government's adopting any extensive scheme for collecting statistical information throughout the country, but had made valuable suggestions as to the type of investigation to which a body of amateur statisticians like the Manchester Society might turn their attention. Their first task might well be to make a classification of the people of Manchester, and to ascertain " the command which in a right state of moral feeling the working classes have over the necessaries of life." Information could be collected as to the prices of provisions and clothes ; and " the consumption of butchers' meat in Manchester would, in connection with that of ardent spirits, form an excellent test of the manner in which the earnings of the poor are expended, and of the degree in which frugality or forethought prevails." The number of cheap publications circulated and their character might serve to indicate " the opinion and the state of feelings in the lower orders " ; and the growth of trade could be suggested by statistics of the horse-power employed in Manchester mills and the tonnage of goods carried by canal and railway over a series of years. Dr. Kay further suggested that information as to the relation of capital to wages and profits might be extracted from the Report of the Factory

Commissioners, and that the Society might appoint a sub-committee to make a digest of that report. Finally, he mentioned that Poulett Thomson had promised to supply the Society with the returns made to the questions issued by the Government on the motion of the Earl of Kerry, concerning the education of the people, so far as Manchester and the adjacent townships were concerned; and these, it was added, might serve as the basis for future inquiry.

How closely the work of the Society during the first seven years conformed to the programme thus laid down will be amply evidenced by what follows.

II

Immediately several Committees of Inquiry were set up. One of these, concerned with the Factory Report, consisted of Samuel and William R. Greg; and in order to understand the attitude of these cotton spinners it is necessary to recall the circumstances in which the Factory Act of 1833 had been passed. In 1831 Michael Sadler had secured a Committee of Inquiry into the State of the Factory Population, the report of which had raised such resentment among the manufacturers that they had demanded the appointment of a Commission to investigate the facts in the manufacturing areas themselves. The report of this Commission led to the passing of the Factory Act of 1833, which fixed the minimum age of employment in textile factories at nine, and limited the hours of work of children and young people under eighteen years of age. The Act, while far from satisfying Sadler, Ashley and the other leaders of the Ten Hours Movement, was intensely unpopular with the employers, and the report of the brothers Greg, which was read to the Society on March 12, concludes:

" that the health and morals of the people employed in cotton mills are at least equal to that of those engaged in other occupations

c

in the towns in which they are situated; that the long hours of labour do *not* over-fatigue the children, or injure their health and constitutions; that the general charges of cruelty and ill-treatment, which have been so repeatedly alleged, are entirely groundless; that the education of the factory children, as compared with others, is more carefully attended to; that the poor rates are lower in Lancashire than in any other county in the kingdom; and that the wages of labour are such as, in the agricultural districts, would be regarded as positive opulence."

The Gregs add that " the inapplicability of the Factory Bill to such a state of things must be evident to all who will compare the two." [1]

Another Committee had the duty of investigating immoral and irreligious publications circulating in Manchester.   Its report is short enough to be reproduced in full :

" About 900 Copies are sold weekly of the *Poor Man's Guardian*, *Dispatch*, *Moral World*, *Police Gazette*, *Political Register* and *Roebuck's Political Pamphlet* at 1*d*. and 2*d*. each.

About 400 Copies are sold weekly of *Paddy Kelly* and *Bob Logic* at 1*d*. each.

About 220 Copies are sold weekly of the *Doctor* at 1*d*. each.

In addition to these, about 600 Copies have been sold during the last twelve months of the *Bridal Gem*, *Fruits of Philosophy* and *Moral Physiology*.

About 400 Copies of Paine's *Age of Reason* and about 200 Copies of other similar works at 6*d*. or 15*d*. each have been sold during the last three years.

About 800 Copies of Paine's *Rights of Man* have been sold during the last three years.

The principal part of the works now mentioned are sold to the Working Classes, excepting *Bob Logic* and *Paddy Kelly*, which are sold almost exclusively to persons employed in Ware-houses.

About 1600 Copies are sold weekly of the *Penny Magazine*, *Saturday's Magazine*, *Dublin Penny Journal* and *Chambers*

---

[1] The analysis was printed (*Guard Book*, p. 5) by order of the Society. Of one witness whose evidence was hostile the authors of the digest remark : " And to put the copestone to his own character and credit, he commenced his evidence by refusing to take the oath—declares that he does not believe in a God—that he formerly lived with Carlile and the Rev. Robert Taylor—and that nevertheless he is a moral character ! "

Journal at 1*d.* and 1*s.* each, but it is impossible to state what number of these are distributed among the Working Classes.

About 500 Copies of the *Penny Story Teller* are weekly sold to the Working Classes.

We have omitted to mention amongst the first list Cobbett's *Legacy to Parsons*, of which about 1800 Copies have been sold during the last six weeks at 1*s.* 6*d.* each."

Copies of the publications that found most favour with the operatives were presented to the Society; and though some, no doubt, disturbed the minds of the statisticians, the annual report registered the opinion " that cheap works of an unexceptionable character are far more extensively circulated than those of an immoral tendency "—a conclusion that may have encouraged members to oppose the Newspaper Stamp Duty, which, after a long agitation, was reduced in 1836 from four-pence to one penny.[1]

Equally informative was the work of the Committee on the use of steam-power, the report of which was presented by Richard Birley[2] in 1837. Full particulars were obtained of every engine at work in certain towns, and the tables prepared by the Committee are eloquent of the extent to which the new source of power was transforming the industrial life of the areas selected. In the year 1836 the aggregate horse-power of steam-engines in Manchester and Salford was 9,924½. In the same year the Bolton district had no fewer than 308 steam engines (ninety of which were used in cotton mills and seventy-eight at coal mines), representing an aggregate of 5,251½ horse-power units. Sixty water-wheels were still at work in the same area (eighteen in cotton mills, and four at collieries) with a total horse-power of 1,171 units.

[1] *Chambers' Journal* had been started by William and Robert Chambers in Edinburgh in 1832; the *Penny Magazine,* founded in the same year, was published by the Society for the Diffusion of Useful Knowledge; and the *Saturday Magazine* was issued by the Society for Promoting Christian Knowledge. Hammond : *The Age of the Chartists*, pp. 314–15.

[2] The Committee consisted of John Kennedy, Henry Houldsworth, Henry McConnel, William Neild, James Murray, Peter Ewart and Richard Birley.

The expansion of steam-power was obviously dependent on supplies of fuel, and a Committee was set up to ascertain the quantity of coal brought into Manchester. James Meadows, who was chiefly responsible for the work of this Committee, reported in 1837 that the tonnage brought into the town was as follows :

1834	737,008
1835	820,000
1836	913,991

It should not, however, be imagined that the increase represented in these figures was the normal rate of growth of coal consumption; for the period was one of rapidly improving trade, and 1836 was followed by some years of trade recession. Both in 1834 and in 1836 the proportion of the coal carried to Manchester by canal was 63 per cent.: the remainder came by turnpike road and rail.[1]

Closely linked with the development of steam-power and coal was the fate of the hand-loom weavers, who formed an important section of the working-class population of South-East Lancashire at this time. On April 23, 1834, Dr. Kay reported that, after several meetings, the Committee set up for the purpose " had been unable to devise any plan by which the investigation of the conditions of that distressed body of artisans could be undertaken as a separate inquiry, without great uncertainty as to the accuracy of the results." It had therefore prepared a form of inquiries for the whole population of an area, and Benjamin Heywood had undertaken to meet the expense of employing an agent to go from door to door to collect the desired information. During the months of May and June 1834, the agent, Mr. Henderson, was at work under the supervision of an official of the District Provident Society, and Mr. Langton and Dr. Kay. The area selected was the Police Division of

[1] The figures were printed. *Miscellaneous Papers*, 1837–61.

St. Michael's (which at the Census of 1831 contained 5,400 families and 25,581 persons) and that part of the Police Division of New Cross which lay between Oldham Road and the Rochdale Canal (containing 3,532 families and 16,554 persons)—a part of the town which, more than any other, was peopled by the working class. The sample taken consisted of almost one in every two houses; and the results of the inquiry were of such interest that they were read twice by Benjamin Heywood before the Statistical Section of the British Association at Edinburgh in 1834. Of the 4,102 families investigated, only 55 per cent. were English, nearly 43 per cent. were Irish, 0·9 per cent. were Welsh, and 0·5 per cent. Scottish. Practically one-half of the families professed adherence to the Established Church, one-third were Roman Catholics, and one-seventh dissenters. Three-quarters of the families lived in houses, a little more than one-twentieth in rooms, and nearly one-fifth in cellars. Little over a third of the dwellings were reported to be " comfortable." Rents varied considerably, but the norm lay between 1s. 6d. and 3s. a week, and relatively few families paid more than 4s. Of 12,117 children only 252 were in attendance at day schools and only 4,680 at Sunday Schools. There were practically two wage-earners to a family on the average; 28 per cent. of the workers were in factories; 27 per cent. were hand-loom weavers; 8 per cent.—mainly winders—were engaged in warehouses; and 8 per cent. in the building trades. The results of the inquiry were ordered to be printed, and the tables were reproduced in the *Manchester Guardian*, the *Courier* and *Wheeler's Manchester Chronicle* in November 1834.

So interesting were the results that it was decided to extend the survey to other areas of Manchester and Salford and the outlying towns of Bury, Ashton, Stalybridge and Dukinfield. During seventeen months of 1834–6 four agents, each paid 16s. a week, were busy making a house-to-house investigation, and a series of reports, all full of detailed figures and written with

entire objectivity, was printed by the Society.[1] Among
the facts brought to light was the superiority of housing
conditions in the new industrial towns to the north and
east over those of the older centres of Manchester and
Liverpool.[2]   In Manchester no fewer than 3,571 cellar
dwellings were discovered with an average of 4·17 persons to a cellar, and the percentage of the population so
housed was estimated at 11¾. In Liverpool things
were still worse, for there about 15 per cent. of the
people were cellar-dwellers. But in Bury, on the other
hand, the percentage was only 3¾ and in Ashton-under-
Lyne 1¼. In Manchester and Salford nearly 28 per
cent. of the houses were reported as "not comfortable"; in Ashton, Dukinfield and Stalybridge less than
5 per cent. were so described by the same investigators.
As would be expected, a higher proportion of the population in the smaller towns was found to be engaged in
manufacture, as distinct from other occupations. In
Manchester and Salford nearly 9 per cent. of those
employed in manufacture were hand-loom weavers; in
Bury less than 6 per cent.; and in Ashton, Dukinfield
and Stalybridge less than 3 per cent. Of heads of
houses and lodgers in Manchester no less than 16 per
cent. were Irish; for Ashton, Dukinfield and Stalybridge
the corresponding figure was 14½ per cent.; and for
Bury only 2·4 per cent. It was to this smaller degree
of colonisation, it may be added, that Dr. Kay[3] attributed
the fact that in some of these smaller towns "the dwellings of the poor contain more furniture, and are cleaner,
and their diet is superior to that of a large proportion
of the population of Manchester."
    Not that the diet of Manchester was, according to

[1] The cost of the inquiry was £175. The *Report on the Condition
of Working Classes in an Extensive Manufacturing District*, which covered
these six towns, was read by W. R. Greg before the Statistical Section
of the British Association at Liverpool in September 1837.
[2] The figures for Liverpool were collected in the course of the inquiry
into the state of education in Liverpool made in 1835–6.
[3] Evidence given before Sir George Cornwall Lewis in 1834. Kay-
Shuttleworth, *Four Periods of Public Education*, p. 153.

the standards of the time, a poor one. A Committee had been set up to ascertain the consumption of meat in the town, and a report was presented by James McConnel in 1837. The Committee had employed a paid agent not only to collect information from butchers and pork-dealers individually, but also, as a check, to ascertain from the tanners and fellmongers, as well as from the Railway Office, the quantity of hides received from butchers. According to their tables the weekly consumption of butchers' meat in Manchester in 1836 was 695,176⅙ lb., or an average of no less than 2 lb. per head of the population.

It was inevitable that the question should be asked as to how far the manufacturing system was responsible for the ills that afflicted the workers. In 1839, therefore, it was decided, for the sake of comparison, to extend the inquiry into the condition of the working classes to a purely agricultural area; and for this purpose three parishes of the county of Rutland were selected. The report on these, which was read before the Statistical Section of the British Association in August 1839, suggests that housing conditions in this rural county were better than those of the towns. The thatched house of the labourer, built of stone, had normally a dairy or storehouse attached, together with a garden big enough to supply a family with vegetables. If the percentage of houses reported as being " well-furnished " and " comfortable " was somewhat lower than in Manchester and Salford, and considerably lower than in Dukinfield, " the general appearance of the interior of the houses indicated thrifty poverty, and instances of the squalid misery so frequent in large towns are here extremely rare." Moreover, overcrowding, as measured by the percentage of families with more than three persons to a bed, was considerably lower and rents were small in comparison with those of Lancashire. Of the moral condition of these rural labourers the Committee formed a favourable impression. " Swearing and drunkenness are far from common, and the general conduct of

the people is marked by sobriety, frugality and industry."
But "their education has been but limited, nor has
their intelligence been very highly developed; and
though few dwellings were entirely without books, these
were found to be far from numerous or well-selected,
and were almost exclusively confined to religious subjects." A labourer whose literary horizon was bounded
by Foxe's *Book of Martyrs* or Venn's *Whole Duty of Man*
may have been highly moral, but would hardly have
the alertness of mind of a town artisan who fed freely
from the hand of Cobbett or Tom Paine.

Similarly, in Hull, where a house-to-house visitation
was made in 1839, the houses were found to be superior
to those of Lancashire; rents were lower, ventilation
was better, the streets were cleaner, and the houses less
frequently built in courts. "While in Liverpool one-
fifth, and in Manchester and Salford one-tenth, of the
working classes were found to be living in cellars, in
Hull there are only fifteen in every 10,000." The
explanation was partly racial: in Hull 95 per cent. of
the heads of families were English, only 2 per cent.
were Irish and $1\frac{1}{2}$ per cent. Scots.[1] Hull showed up
well, moreover, in the matter of juvenile labour; of
those under twenty-one years only 21 per cent. were
employed for wages, against 35 per cent. in Manchester
and Salford, and 40 per cent. in Ashton and Dukinfield.
And a similarly lower proportion of women in paid
employment meant that the mothers were able to give
full attention to their households. In one important
respect, however, conditions were little, if any, better
than in the manufacturing towns. "It appears that
in 29 per cent., or not far from one-third of the ascertained cases, there were more than three individuals to

[1] These figures are from the *Report on the State of Education in Kingston-
upon-Hull*. How far Irish overcrowding was due to poverty and how
far to other characteristics of the immigrants is difficult to determine.
After referring to an instance of a house that sheltered twenty Irish,
G. S. Kenrick adds that "the inhabitants of the Sister Isle are so
gregarious that it is difficult to separate them into small families." (*The
Population of Pontypool Situated in the so-called Disturbed Districts*.)

one bed; that in 13 per cent. there were five and upwards; and in 103 cases, seven and upwards to one
bed!"[1]

The work of these Committees, no doubt, stimulated
individual members to make surveys of particular areas
in which they were personally interested. The earliest
of these was that made by Benjamin Heywood in 1835
for the village of Irlams-o'-th'-Height, which showed,
among other things, that out of 389 persons in receipt
of wages no fewer than 169 were hand-loom weavers.
The depressed situation of these is revealed in the fact
that, whereas at the boys' day school the normal weekly
charge was threepence for reading only and fourpence
for reading, writing and arithmetic, the children of hand-
loom weavers were admitted at a charge of a penny a
week. Another investigation of the same character was
that of James Heywood into the state of 176 families in
Miles Platting, where in 1837 (a year of severe depression) " many of the hand-loom weavers . . . did not
find half employment; others were unable to earn more
than 6s. or 7s. per week, and the most experienced and
industrious of the class, by working fourteen hours per
day, frequently obtained for the full amount of their
earnings only 12s. per week."[2]

But perhaps the most exhaustive study of an area by
a single person was that of the parish of Alderley made
by the Rev. Edward Stanley in 1836. His report gives
figures not only of dwellings and people, of literates and
illiterates, but also of Bibles and Prayer-Books (an
average of two of each per house), of church and sacra-
mental attendances, of occupations, of agricultural stock
and implements, of horses, cows, pigs, sheep, fowls,
geese, ducks, turkeys, pigeons and beehives: one is
left wondering at the omission of a census of the bees
themselves.

[1] *Report on the Condition of the Working Classes in Kingston-upon-Hull*,
p. 5.   [2] *Journal of the Statistical Society of London*, Vol. I, p. 34.

III

It was natural that one of the first problems to which members addressed themselves should have been that of Education. For it was just a few days before the birth of the Society—on August 17, 1833—that the first modest grant of £20,000 was made by the Treasury to the British and Foreign School Society and its larger rival the National Society for Promoting the Education of the Poor in the Principles of the Established Church. The meeting of January 7, 1835, which was attended by Poulett Thomson, was largely occupied with the question of religious teaching: Dr. Kay read a paper on " The Means Existing for the Religious Instruction of the Working Classes in Large Towns "; W. R. Greg submitted a table of the number of churches and chapels-of-ease in each county; and William Langton presented tables and maps showing the local distribution of places of worship and Sunday Schools. From these it appeared that in the area of Manchester and Salford (with a population, in 1831, of 226,964) there were twenty-one churches, forty-eight dissenting chapels, and four Catholic chapels; the number of Sunday Schools was 108 and of scholars 40,934. The most important point brought out by Langton was the relative scarcity of places of worship and Sunday Schools in the newer industrial areas to the north and east of the two towns. As the result of the discussion that followed, a Committee of four clergymen and four laymen was appointed to carry out an inquiry into the facilities for religious instruction in the district. This very tactfully issued two questionnaires, one to the clergy, the others to ministers of religion. But, in spite of all precautions, the inquiry met with much suspicion and hostility; and one reverend gentleman in Salford told the Committee roundly that " no end could be answered by the inquiry but the gratification of their impertinent curiosity." It was by no means the only time that members were abused for

venturing into a field which the Churches regarded as
their own.

More success attended the researches of a Committee
set up in April 1834 to investigate the state of public and
private education in Manchester. In order to appreciate
the circumstances in which the inquiry was made, it is
necessary to recall that the Earl of Kerry—who, it will be
remembered, had attended an early meeting of the Society
—had recently moved in Parliament for a return on the
present state of education in England. Rickman, who
had been responsible for the Census of 1831, distributed
some 15,000 circulars to the overseers throughout the
country; and on the basis of the statistics collected it was
estimated that 1,276,947 children (or one in eleven of the
total population) were attending day schools, and
1,548,890 (or one in nine of the population) were in
attendance at Sunday Schools.[1]

" It was the feeling that justice was not done in these
returns to efforts made by the friends of education among
the manufacturers of Lancashire," wrote G. R. Porter,[2]
" that incited the Statistical Society of Manchester to set
on foot the extensive series of inquiries which, with their
results, they subsequently gave to the public." No
fewer than seventeen members of the Society took part
in the local inquiry, but a full-time paid agent, James
Riddall Wood, was chiefly responsible for the collection
of data. The report on Manchester, which was prepared
by Samuel Greg, was presented on July 1, 1835. It
points out that 21·6 per cent. of the total population of
the town were receiving instruction, and that about
10 per cent. were attending day and evening schools.
If attention were confined to children between the ages
of five and fifteen, about two-thirds would be found to be
obtaining education of one sort or other. The investigation showed that the returns made under the Earl of
Kerry's motion were seriously deficient, and that no
fewer than 181 schools and 8,000 to 9,000 scholars

[1] Hammond, *The Age of the Chartists*, pp. 180–81.
[2] *Progress of the Nation* (ed. 1847), p. 702.

had been omitted for the township of Manchester alone.

Of the schools themselves much information is given. At one dame school eleven children were found in a small room in which the mistress was lying in bed suffering from measles and in which a child had died of the same disease a few days before; and at another twenty children were obliged to squat on the floor, since there was no furniture of any kind in the room. At one common day school the investigator met the master issuing from his schoolroom at the head of his scholars to see a fight in the neighbourhood. But of the infant schools the Committee speak highly: " Their design and management are excellent, and their general utility likely to be very great."

The Report concludes that the means of education in Manchester are " extremely inadequate," that it is desirable that infant schools should gradually supplant the old dame schools, that no effectual means can be taken to render the common day schools efficient " until proper seminaries are established for the instruction of the teachers themselves, and till the idea is exploded that the task of education is the only one for which no previous knowledge or qualification is required." At the request of the Earl of Kerry, a copy of the Report was sent in 1835 to the Committee of the House of Commons on the State of Education in the Kingdom, and the investigation attracted so much attention that it was decided to extend it to other towns. A report on Bury, published a few months later in 1835, revealed a less unsatisfactory state of affairs: of an estimated number of 5,000 children between the ages of five and fifteen, only 700 were receiving no instruction whatsoever; there were more Sunday School teachers; and the conditions of the schools were better than in Manchester. Again errors were discovered in the Government returns, which gave only fifty-four schools with 5,558 scholars, whereas the Society found seventy-three schools and 6,419 scholars.

The Report on Salford, published in 1836, follows

similar lines. For the numbers under instruction comparison with Manchester was "in a trifling degree favourable to Salford." Reference is again made to the incompetence and poverty of the teachers ; the suggestion is put forward "that in the establishment of normal schools, the funds devoted to educational purposes would be more usefully employed, than in any other manner " ; and—in a footnote, it is true—the daring question is raised whether the instruction of the rising generation ought to be left any longer to the sole caprice of the parents.[1]

Two and a half years later the Society decided to make a more minute study of the educational facilities in part of Salford, and a house-to-house visitation was made in the township of Pendleton. Comparison with the figures of the earlier Report suggested that the depression of trade (which had fallen, it was remarked, most heavily on those *least* dependent on the steam-engine) had led to a fall in the numbers attending the common schools and dame schools. Whereas for Salford as a whole, in 1835, six-tenths of the children aged five to fifteen were not attending day or evening school, in Pendleton in 1838 the proportion was one-half. Since only about $2\frac{1}{2}$ to 3 per cent. of the children of the township appeared to be left entirely uneducated, it followed that the average period of instruction must have been very short. Of the children who had left school, the Report revealed that only a third had remained there more than five years ; and that of the remainder half had attended for less than three years. Among other conclusions was "that the humbler schools are ephemeral and inefficient " ; and

---

[1] In a MS. report laid before the Society on January 6, 1836, the Committee aggregate the summary figures for Manchester and Salford :

"1. It appears that in these Boroughs at least 20,000 children between five and fifteen are under no course of instruction.

"2. That out of the total number of 56,189 scholars (44,000 of whom are computed to be between five and fifteen) 26,660 attend day and evening schools, one half of this number going at the same time to Sunday Schools.

"3. 29,529 receive no other instruction than that of Sunday Schools."

that at least one-half of the children of the working classes
were exceedingly irregular in attendance.   Generally the
autobiographical detail collected was not flattering to the
schools.   One labourer remarked that " one lad teached
another all that was taught "; and a woman told the
visitor that " the mistress used to set the scholars agate
o' peeling potatoes and fetching water 'stead of teaching
them to read."   Incidentally the Report throws light on
other social conditions in the area : while in Manchester
and Salford the Irish constituted 16 per cent. of the
population, in Pendleton they were not more than 2 or
3 per cent.—a difference the Committee put down to
the fact that poor relief was not given to the Irish in
the township, as it was in Manchester.   Whereas of the
handloom weavers in Manchester probably nearly half
were Irish, among 338 adult handloom weavers and
winders in Pendleton only four Irish were found.   The
Committee called attention to the lack of ventilation in
many of the houses and cellars, to the overcrowding of
bedrooms, and to the imperfection of the system of
drainage—a matter that was to occupy much of the
Society's time during the next few years.

In the session 1836–7 the Education Committee
presented a report on the state of education in Liverpool,
which had been prepared by Henry Romilly, W. R. Greg
and William Langton.   Once more it was found that
" of the whole number of children in the Borough of an
age to be instructed, more than one-half are receiving no
education in schools, either really or nominally."   The
circumstances in which those receiving nominal instruction were taught were sometimes deplorable :

"In a garret up three pairs of broken stairs was a common
day school, with forty children, in the compass of ten feet by nine.
On a perch, forming a triangle with the corner of the room, sat
a cock and two hens; under a stump bed, immediately beneath,
was a dog kennel, in the occupation of three black terriers, whose
barking, added to the noise of the children and the cackling of the
fowls, on the approach of a stranger, were almost deafening.
There was only one small window, at which sat the master,

obstructing three-fourths of the light it was capable of admitting.
. . . Another school is worthy of description. The descent
is by a flight of narrow steps, fifteen inches in width, and covered
with filth; the room is naturally dark, but it is rendered doubly so
from the dirt without and the steam within the windows; the
forms are composed of four old bedstocks, resting on brick supports;
the writing-desk is a three-legged table or stool, accommodating
only one scholar at a time. The master, an Irishman, represented
himself as a ' graduate of the University of Munster, the first
place for scholarship in all Ireland.' "

There was in Liverpool the same ignorance and
poverty of teachers as in Manchester: ten mistresses of
dame schools acknowledged to being in receipt of assistance from the poor rate, and the average income of 244
such schools was little over 6s. a week. The only
important difference between conditions here and those
in Manchester and Salford lay in the larger part played
by day schools, and the smaller part by Sunday Schools
in Liverpool: [1] a difference a later writer explained by
the greater development of the factory system in Manchester, which made attendance at day schools impossible
for many children.[2]

A similar inquiry was made in the same year by Henry
and Edmund Ashworth into the state of education in
Bolton, and the report of this was read before the Statistical Section of the British Association at Liverpool in
1837. The position disclosed was even less satisfactory
than that in Manchester and Salford; for not only were
nearly 30 per cent. of the children without any schooling
whatsoever, but more than two-thirds of the scholars
attended Sunday School only. As in other areas,
" necessity, not fitness, seems in almost every instance to
have been the cause of the teachers' adopting this employment "; and one woman said that she had become a
teacher because she could not weave, and another that

[1] The day scholars in Liverpool bore to those in Manchester and
Salford the proportion of 126 to 97, and the Sunday scholars that of 67
to 168¾.

[2] T. R. Wilkinson, " Report upon the Educational Conditions of
Gaythorn and Knott Mill," *Transactions*, 1867–8, p. 54.

she had taken to the calling because she " geet poor and war a widow."

As with the investigation into the condition of the working classes, so with the education inquiry it seemed important to discover how far similar defects were to be found in areas where manufacture was not the dominant activity. As an archiepiscopal city, with a relatively small working-class population and many educational endowments, York seemed one suitable field for this purpose; and the parishes of Rutlandshire and the town of Hull offered other types of non-industrial communities. As might have been expected, the proportion of children who attended school free of charge was found to be much higher in York than in Manchester, and 67 per cent. of the children between the ages of five and fifteen were at school. " The palm must be conceded to York and Rutland," wrote the Committee, " over either Manchester and Salford or Liverpool; for though inferior to Manchester in the number and efficiency of the Sunday Schools, they supply a more general day school instruction than is found to exist in Manchester by at least 50 per cent.; and although not more than 20 or 30 per cent. better than Liverpool in the relative number of day schools, yet the Sunday-School instruction is in more than double the proportion." Most of the schools in York were better than those of the industrial towns, but there were the same mistaken methods of teaching. " The Bible (or parts of it) is the general book from which the alphabet is learned, amid much flagellation and many tears," and " Religion is taught by the catechism, and morals by the rod."

Hull showed a proportion of day scholars to population approximately the same as that of York and Rutland; and an inquiry as to the ability of adults to read, write and cipher, was favourable to Hull as compared with Pendleton. The Committee concluded that " the working classes in Hull seem to have a just appreciation of the value of education, as well those parents who have been deprived of the advantages of instruction as those

who have been more favourably circumstanced "—
though there were exceptions like the " respectable
female " who had not allowed her daughters to learn to
write, " because it would only set them writing love-
letters."

The inquiries into the state of education had arisen
out of a legitimate criticism of Rickman's figures. They
showed that, for the areas investigated, the omissions
in Parliamentary returns were about one-third of the
actual number of scholars. But it is manifest that their
function far exceeded that of mere correction ; and it
would be difficult to over-estimate the part played by
the reports in awakening the social conscience not only
of the communities concerned, but of the nation at large.
For since most of them were read before the British
Association, and several were given in evidence before
Government committees, they had wide publicity. Subsequent inquiries made by the statisticians of London
were based on them.[1] And though the conclusion
reached, and expressed in the last paragraph of the report
on Liverpool, aroused some dissent when it was read at
the British Association, it was the one to which the logic
of events was forcing the minds of most thoughtful
observers of the new industrial society. " We feel
persuaded," wrote W. R. Greg and William Langton,
who were responsible for the paragraph, " that the
establishment of a Board of Public Instruction would be
hailed by all who have seen the glaring deficiencies of
the present state of education as the first step in the
performance of a duty, which is imperative with every
enlightened government." To make Britain take that
first, and several succeeding steps, was to be the life-
work of their colleague, Kay-Shuttleworth.

[1] See G. R. Porter, *Progress of the Nation* (ed. 1847), p. 702; Sect.
VII., Ch. IV., p. 695.

CHAPTER III

MORTALITY TABLES AND RAILWAY LABOUR

To write a consecutive history of the activities of the Society during the forties is impossible; for with the Session 1839–40 the series of annual reports (which William Langton had carefully preserved) cease; and it is not until 1853 that the regular publication of *Transactions* begins. For the intervening years we have the titles of most of the papers; but of their contents we know little, except in the case of one or two that were specially printed by order of the Society.

The period opened with high promise. At the seventh annual meeting, in October 1840, no fewer than six committees were set up to carry out such varied tasks as gathering statistics of the cotton industry; obtaining annual figures of births, marriages and deaths in Manchester and Salford; drawing up tables of the prices of meat and bread supplied to the Infirmary, College and Workhouse; inquiring into the cases of those admitted to the Night Asylum; procuring a statement of goods brought into and sent out of Manchester by canal and railway; and preparing an account of popular outbreaks and commotions in the town since the setting up of the first local newspaper.

How many of these bodies carried their work to fruition it is not possible to say. But one at least—that concerned with births, marriages and deaths—produced a report of the utmost value. The project of preparing accurate annual bills of mortality in Manchester was no new one; for as early as 1775 proposals to this end had been made by Dr. Percival, and subscriptions had been obtained from a number of men who afterwards became members of

34

the Literary and Philosophical Society.[1] In 1786 Thomas Henry made some " Observations on the Bills of Mortality for the Towns of Manchester and Salford," in which he showed that, contrary to what was believed to be true of London, the population of these towns was increasing rapidly. It was true that as Manchester grew the proportion of people who lived to old age fell.

" But injurious as large towns may be to the duration of life, and though it must be granted that by annually draining the country of a number of inhabitants, they consume many lives, which in their original situation might have continued to exist for several years longer, but are cut off by diseases produced by vitiated air, by infection, or by a change in their modes of living, yet, on the whole, they are not, perhaps, so unfavourable to population as they may, at first sight, appear. For in large towns, at least in those where extensive manufactures are carried on, the encourage-ments to matrimony are considerable; and therefore, if life be more speedily wasted, it is probably produced in a far greater ratio. A sensible, industrious manufacturer considers his children as his treasure, and boasts that his quiver is full of them; for where children can be employed at an early age, the fear of a large family is not only diminished, but every child that is born may be regarded as an addition to fortune." [2]

The three members of the Society who were deputed to carry out the new investigation had the co-operation of the local registrars of births, marriages and deaths who had been appointed under the Registration Act of 1837 ; and they were assisted, moreover, by at least three paid investigators.[3] The inquiry was confined to the eight townships of Manchester, Hulme, Salford,

[1] R. Angus Smith, " A Centenary of Science in Manchester," *Memoirs of the Literary and Philosophical Society of Manchester* (Third Series), Vol. IX., p. 35.

[2] Quoted, *ibid.*, pp. 119–20.

[3] Letters from members of the Committee are preserved asking William Langton to pay men of the names of Johns, Latham and Young-man an aggregate of £20 for help in preparing Mortality Bills during the months of July, August and September 1840. The Manchester inquiry may have owed something to James Cleland of Glasgow, a Corresponding Member, who had presented a copy of his *Historical Account of Bills of Mortality in Glasgow and Other Towns* on its publication in 1836.

Pendleton, Ardwick, Chorlton-upon-Medlock, Broughton and Cheetham (with Crumpsall) which together, in 1841, contained a population of 305,933. Of these townships the first four were peopled chiefly by the poorer operatives ; they had the largest number of courts and cellar dwellings ; and, since the factories and workshops were clustered thickly along the rivers and canals that passed through them, the inhabitants lived under an almost perpetual cloud of smoke. Between 1801 and 1841 their population had increased nearly three-fold, from 89,308 to 255,070. They represented by far the greater part of the population of Manchester and Salford.

Ardwick and Chorlton-upon-Medlock attracted the growing body of the more skilled and better-paid operatives. During the same period their numbers had increased more than fifteen-fold, from 2,437 to 38,242. Cheetham and Broughton were the homes of the well-to-do classes and were still relatively sparsely populated ; they had grown from 2,070 in 1801 to 12,621 in 1841.

The effect of these factors on births and deaths is summarised in the following figures for three of the townships in 1841.

	Manchester.	C.-on-M.	Broughton.
Proportion of births to population one in	24·75	25·25	33·57
Proportion of illegitimate to total births one in	17·93	25·50	56·50
Proportion of deaths to population one in	31·59	39·30	68·98

The report is illustrated with maps, and includes meteorological statistics based on the work of John Dalton, as well as an account of the geology of the district contributed by Edward Binney, secretary of the Manchester Geological Society. Its tables abound with information for the social historian. The extent of education among adults, for example, can be gathered from the statement that of those who married in 1841 the percentage who were unable to write was, for males, 25·9, and for females 57·5. But, most of all, the report is valuable for its account of the way in which industrial development was sundering what had previously been a homogeneous community:

"Owing to the increasing annoyance of smoke, the noise and bustle of business, and perhaps also the growing value of building land, for shops and warehouses in the central parts, all the families of the comfortable class, whose avocations or circumstances permit a change of residence, have in the course of the last few years removed from the township of Manchester and almost to an equal extent from that of Salford, to the outer townships; whereby large tracts of the town remain occupied solely by operatives. This change, though it may promote the health of the families of the opulent, is to be regarded as unfavourable to the town as a community; since it has drawn a broad line of separation as to residence between the employers and the employed, which in the issue must prove equally inimical to the well-being of both. But the increase of smoke threatens to extend the same evil until it may happen that the operatives in all are deserted by the superior class . . . in ten years hence it would seem far from improbable that most of the comfortable class will have withdrawn from the town (except perhaps the outer margins of three or four out of the eight townships), and consequently that a mass of operatives, falling little short of three hundred thousand, will be left to dwell by themselves, subject to the various evils incident to a great community, the component parts of which are so ill arranged and so unnaturally sundered and disjoined."

A Report on the Vital Statistics of Manchester was presented to the Statistical Section of the British Association [1] at its Manchester meeting in 1841; and that the problems arising out of the labours of the Committee continued to occupy the minds of members for several years is evidenced by the titles of papers read before the Society.[2] The Report itself was presented by John Roberton in the session 1843–4.

[1] A reference to this is made in Cooke-Taylor, *Manufacturing District of Lancashire* (1842), p. 264.
[2] In the session 1841–2 W. R. Greg read a paper " On the Change in the Rate of Mortality in England " and John Roberton followed with

Roberton was a Scottish doctor who had been appointed surgeon to the Manchester Lying-in Hospital in 1827. Joining the Society as an ordinary member in 1838, he had been appointed a member of the Executive Committee in the following year, and was President from 1844 to 1847. Between 1834 and 1865 he read to the members no fewer than twenty-seven papers on topics that ranged from " The Medical Statistics of the Negro Race " and " The Physiology of the Hindoos " to " The Influence of Land Tenure on Cultivation " and " The Best Means of Improving the Climate of Manchester." He had many bees in his Scottish bonnet: an ardent believer in the peasant ownership of the soil, he set forth his views on primogeniture and entail in a paper (on which, however, his name does not appear), specially printed by order of the Society in 1851. Another of his preoccupations was the surplus of women. In one of the earliest of his contributions, made in 1840, he argued " that as this excess is produced by causes which remain in steady operation, we detect therein a natural law, and may allowably infer that it exists for beneficial social ends." He concluded that " the female sex, in Christian countries, are probably designed for duties more in numbers and in importance than have yet been assigned to them." Lest it be thought that Mr. Roberton was a spiritual ancestor of another member of the Society, Dr. Pankhurst, let it be added that he did not contemplate the election of women to the town council, but merely wished to see set up " a committee of ladies in each ward out of the families employing labour therein, to co-operate with the authorities for the welfare of the people drawn thither to produce the wealth which gives to the families in question their subsistence and their position in society."

Perhaps the greatest single service rendered by

" A Preface to the Report of the Registration Committee." In the following session P. H. Holland read a paper " On the Medical Inspection of Towns and the Registration of the Causes of Death."

Roberton, however, was to call the attention of members to the conditions of life of the navvies and labourers who were bringing into being the system of British railways. After the lull that followed the boom of 1836–7 construction had been resumed on a large scale; and between 1843 and 1846 thousands of miles of rail were laid down. So active were the projectors that it has been said that in the last of these years at least one Bill for a new railway was passed on every parliamentary day.[1] The work of construction required large masses of able-bodied labour, and this was drawn largely from the rural areas of Britain and from Ireland. Expert navigators, assisted by less skilled labourers, were assembled in gangs by undertakers and contractors, who frequently let out part of the work to sub-contractors ; and, as in mining and agriculture, sub-contracting in railway work was almost inevitably associated with the truck-system, and with long intervals between pay days. Equally serious was the problem of housing. Here and there the battalions of navvies could find some sort of accommodation in the villages ; elsewhere the contractors threw up rough huts of stone, wood or turf ; but in either case there was almost always serious overcrowding.

At a meeting of the Society in the Session 1845–6 John Roberton read a paper " On Some of the Evils Affecting the Labourers Engaged in Railway Construction," which described the conditions of life of the men who were boring the Summit Tunnel on the Manchester and Sheffield Railway beneath the moors of Woodhead. According to this, no fewer than thirty-two lives had been lost in the operations.

" ' A serious proportion of the accidents (writes Mr. Roberton) was owing to the men going to work more or less in a state of intoxication.' They were without religious instruction or the means of public worship; their wages paid once in nine weeks; as many as fourteen or fifteen men were lodged in the same rude hut; their money wages, though high, were diminished in value

[1] Clapham, *An Economic History of Modern Britain. The Early Railway Age*, p. 394.

by reason of the prevalence of the truck system; the men were exceedingly drunken and dissolute; and generally the people, men and women, were thoroughly depraved, degraded and reckless.

"Mr. Roberton adds that it must not be supposed that the evils are confined to the Summit Tunnel. ' Let only the existing manner of employing labour and dealing with the labourers in railway construction continue for a few years longer, and we shall have the entire community, from Cornwall to the Orkneys, swarming with tens of thousands of men, and, I will add, women and children, as destitute of religious and moral knowledge, or of sense of duty and propriety, as hordes of Indian savages, and where is he who will then be bold enough to devise, or if devised, to apply the remedy ? ' "[1]

Roberton's paper took the form of a letter addressed to Edwin Chadwick, who was at this time Secretary to the Poor Law Commission. Though Manchester-born, Chadwick was not a member of the Society ; but his wife was the daughter of John Kennedy, and his sister-in-law had married Samuel Robinson. His response to Roberton's appeal was immediate, and on January 22 he came to address the members, along with Robert Rawlinson, the engineer to the Bridgewater Trust, and afterwards a Corresponding Member of the Society. Two days later the following paragraphs appeared in the *Manchester Guardian* :

"Though it is not our custom to publish the proceedings of this Society, the papers read on Thursday evening last were of so interesting and important a character, that we shall make an exception to our usual course. The title of the first paper was ' Descriptive Remarks Relating to Railway Contracts and Railway Workmen,' by Robert Rawlinson, Esq., engineer. The second was entitled ' Memoranda of Facts and Suggestions in Respect of Measures for the Prevention of the Evils Attendant on the Want of Regulations as to the Mode of Employing and Paying Labourers on Railways,' by Edwin Chadwick, Esq., secretary of the poor-law commission. Mr. P. H. Holland, one of the Secretaries of the Society, reminded the members of the letter read at the previous meeting by Mr. Roberton the president, addressed to Mr. Chadwick, descriptive of the condition and

---

[1] *Manchester Guardian*, February 29, 1846.

treatment of railway labourers, especially of those recently employed in the formation of the summit level tunnel on the Sheffield railway. The three papers must be taken as parts of the same. It appears from the evidence contained in them, that the construction of railways, as at present conducted, is accompanied with very great risk to the men engaged; that the losses in killed and wounded are nearly proportional to the losses of an army in a campaign; that the men are crowded together to an undue and injurious extent; that their moral condition is most deplorable, especially as regards sexual immorality and drunkenness; that there is much vagabondage among the class; and that there is great reason to fear that, when these works are discontinued, the dispersion of such a class among the general community will be attended with similar mischief as the disbanding of a small army. At the summit level tunnel the killed may be stated at 3, and the wounded at 14 per cent. The killed (according to the official returns) in the three battles of Talavera, Salamanca and Waterloo, were only 2·11 per cent. of the privates; and in the last forty-one months of the Peninsular War, the privates killed in battle were 4·2 per cent., and by disease 11·9 per cent.

" The maintenance of the families and widows of the men who are killed or maimed is thrown upon the ratepayers of the parishes where they have settlements. There can be no doubt that many of the accidents, attended with fatal results, might be avoided with increased care, and that the expenses caused by those that are purely and strictly accidental ought to be borne by those who profit by the work, not by those who have nothing to do with it, and who can adopt no measures of precaution. Mr. Chadwick suggests that the proprietors of the railways, and through them the contractors, should be made primarily responsible for the losses caused by accidents, however arising. . . . It was stated that a large proportion of the accidents at the summit tunnel had happened from the drunkenness either of the sufferers or of their fellow-workmen. The precaution of preventing any man working while drunk would at once be adopted if it were the contractors' evident interest to be very careful. . . . The contractors or sub-contractors have often an interest in the sale of drink; and sometimes they even pay wages in ' drink tickets ' instead of money. But even allowing that the accidents are the men's own fault— that they do arise entirely or principally from their carelessness or recklessness—the proposed responsibility would at once diminish the value of the careless and reckless workman, and would practically act as a premium upon carefulness and sobriety. In Prussia, a similar plan has long been in operation, as regards the men working in mines; and the results are reported to have been satisfactory.

There, deductions, proportionate to the wages, are made to constitute a fund, in case of accident or death. . . .

" In consequence of a large number of men employed on one spot, and the already crowded state of the cottages of the scattered agricultural population, it generally happens that the house accommodation is very inadequate; what happens is that, first as many of the workmen procure lodgings among the residents as can possibly be taken in, and far more than can be properly or even safely accommodated; the rest erect for themselves temporary abodes of the rudest description, often little better than mud hovels. Sometimes, indeed, the accommodation is so scanty that the men are divided into night and day gangs, in order that one set of beds may serve for two sets of men. As a natural, nay almost inevitable consequence of such overcrowding, the common decencies of life are grossly disregarded, and the condition of the women may be imagined, but cannot be described in any language suitable for publication. ' Their morals,' says Mr. Rawlinson, ' are hopelessly corrupted, and the characters of the males are brutalised. No part of the world can show a more degraded, beastly association of human beings than communities of men and women so situated.' Mr. Chadwick suggests that applicants for a railway Bill should be required to show that there is, or that there will be, provided adequate accommodation for the men who are employed, and that effectual measures be taken to secure the health, comfort and decent separation of the sexes among the numerous people who will be temporarily engaged at a distance from their usual places of abode, and then these large works will be a blessing to the neighbourhoods in which they are carried on."

Edwin Chadwick proposed not only that the employers should be made financially responsible for all accidents, but also—as we should expect of one who had been primarily responsible for the appointment of the first factory inspectors in 1833—that railway works should be subject to public inspection and report. Incidentally, he paid a high tribute to the quality of the local supplies of labour :

" The strongest and most distinguished of the class of navigators . . . are collected principally from the mills in Lancashire and Yorkshire, and are men of the finest physical stamina in the country. In strength and energy they have been exceeded by none in the United Kingdom, and equalled by none on the Continent, and have been toiled after in vain by Norman, German and modern Saxon labourers, who have failed to justify any claims to the same rate of wages. At present on the average they are stated not to last beyond their fortieth year; but with fair treatment they would last with health and vigour their term of three score."[1]

The publication by the Society of the three papers called forth a vigorous reply from Thomas Nicholson, a contractor of Woodhead,[2] who had superintended the work at the Summit Tunnel for three and a half years, during the sinking of the shafts, and had afterwards contracted for the execution of part of the tunnel. Asserting that most of the accidents were the result of the men's own carelessness and disobedience of instructions, he gives a detailed list of the casualties, with particulars of the circumstances in which each occurred. According to his statement, the Statistical Society was in error in putting the number of killed at thirty-two ; only twenty-six men lost their lives, and this was less than the numbers killed on other works of similar magnitude. As to the truck system, he states that when he began the works there were small shops at the west end of the tunnel which sold inferior bacon and sugar, but the results were so unsatisfactory that he set up a provision shop to supply the men. There were inns at Saltersbrook and Dunford Bridge, but no beer tickets were ever issued, except for extra services or wet working ; and he encouraged brewing at home by the sale of malt. A sick club, to which the men each contributed sixpence a week, paid out 8s. a week to each sick member, and bore the expense of funerals. As to the charges of demoralisation, " Does the writer of the pamphlet suppose, then," asks Nicholson, " that these men come to the wilderness of Woodhead, on the mountains of the Sheffield and Manchester Railway, to get religious instruction and education ? . . . You might as well try to stem the tide, as to cultivate a number of men so collected ; because one-third of those men may leave

[1] *Manchester Guardian*, March 7, 1846.
[2] *Strictures on a Pamphlet Published at the Request of the Manchester Statistical Society*, by Thomas Nicholson, 1846.

the works at any day, and a fresh set take their places."
At least they were better off than the pauper agriculturists
in the Andover Workhouse [1]—this was a dig at Chadwick—who had been driven by hunger to gnaw the
putrid flesh and marrow of the bones that had been
given them to grind as a form of task work. " There is
five hundred per cent. more filth and debauchery in
those places in Manchester than you can find in the
worst hut of those which have been so much magnified
at Woodhead. . . . Let the members of the Statistical
Society clear the cobwebs of their own houses, skim
the beam from immediately under their own eyes, before
they send their missionary to discover the mote in another man's." And, finally, " I would strongly recommend Mr. Chadwick to confine his talents and abilities
to the profession he understands, and not to interfere
with engineers, contractors, etc., of tunnels and other
works." But the Committee on Railway Labourers,
before which both Rawlinson and Chadwick gave
evidence, held that they were right. Its report, which
was published in the summer of 1846, and was obviously
greatly influenced by Chadwick, condemned truck,
advocated compulsory weekly payment in cash, declared
in favour of employers' liability, and urged that navvies
should not be brought together till adequate provision
for lodging had been provided.[2] Once again the
private inquiries of the Statistical Society had fore-
shadowed the findings of an official investigation, and
paved the way to reform.

[1] For the Andover Workhouse scandal see B. L. Hutchins, *The Public
Health Agitation*, p. 55, and Hammond, *The Age of the Chartists*, pp.
68–9.

[2] Clapham, *op. cit.*, pp. 410–11.   The Select Committee was appointed
on April 30, 1846.

CHAPTER IV

THE PUBLIC HEALTH CONTROVERSY

THE year 1853 saw the beginning of the *Transactions*; and for the rest of the Society's history the annalist suffers not poverty of means, but the embarrassment of riches. It is impossible to mention more than a small proportion of the papers : all that is attempted is to call attention to the chief topics of discussion, and to make an anthology of paragraphs from contributions that marked the advance of knowledge or were important in directing policy. The reader who has special interest in any one subject can satisfy his curiosity, with the help of the Indexes, by going to the *Transactions* themselves.

During the early fifties perhaps the most debated topic was that of public health : it was the era of the Sanitary Idea. In 1842 Edwin Chadwick had presented to the Poor Law Commission his celebrated *Report on the Sanitary Condition of the Labouring Population of Great Britain*; and in 1844 the Health of Towns Commission had published the recommendations that led to the Public Health Act of 1848, and the creation of the Central Board of Health. With this main current of national life the Statistical Society ran a parallel course. Of 122 papers read between 1853 and 1875 no fewer than one-third were on sanitary and Poor Law subjects, and more than half of these were contributed by medical men.[1] At a period before the birth of bacteriological science, legitimate grounds existed for differences as to the " causes " of the epidemics that

---

[1] T. R. Wilkinson, Presidential Address, *Trans.*, 1875–6.

from time to time swept across the community. There were members of the Society who, like Chadwick, placed emphasis on the part played by dirt in the causation of disease, and there were those who, repelled by Chadwick's undisguised contempt for the medical profession, laid stress on other factors.

In the first group, it is true, were many doctors, of whom John Roberton was perhaps the most prominent. Roberton's association with Chadwick in the inquiry into railway labour has already been described: his later papers abound with ideas in harmony with those of the Central Board of Health. A keen advocate of the use of municipal institutions as a means of social betterment, he urged[1] with vigour the demolition of " honey-comb " or back-to-back dwellings, the setting up of publicly-owned crèches, wash-houses and baths,[2] the municipalisation of hospitals, and—a reform that was to come only three-quarters of a century later—the transfer to the local councils of the functions of Poor Law guardians. His belief in the need for improved drainage found expression in a paper the title of which has aroused much curiosity among members of a later generation: it was " The Best Method of Improving the Climate of Manchester." Since this was read before 1853, and was (so far as can be discovered) never printed, speculation as to the contents is justified. But a search of the files of the *Manchester Guardian* has brought to light a sub-title that suggests Roberton's remedy: it was no other than the tile-drainage of the suburbs. Let anyone who thinks this a matter of small importance refer to those who have lived long enough to remember the mists that used to rise from the ground of Manchester in the evening following a day of heat. The reform advocated by Roberton has played its part in

---

[1] " Suggestions for the Improvement of Municipal Government in Populous Manufacturing Towns," April, 1853.

[2] A paper on " Baths and Wash-Houses for the People " was contributed in the same session by E. T. Bellhouse, who also read a paper on the same subject, twenty-four years later.

giving the town a climate that is now by common consent (of Manchester men) superior to that of the Metropolis.

But perhaps the chief of Roberton's interests was ventilation. It was evidently the experience of the British troops in the Crimean War that drew his attention to the subject, for it was in March 1856 that he read the first of a series of papers with special reference to the ventilation of hospitals.[1] These are of a technical character, and an attempt to summarise them would weary the reader. Suffice it to register the opinion of the architect, Thomas Worthington, " that probably few men in this kingdom have exercised a wider influence over public opinion on hospital construction than Mr. Roberton." [2] In later papers the writer examined the problem of supplies of air in the deep Cornish mines, and applied his principles of ventilation to houses, schools, public buildings, and warehouses.[3]

To the same body of reformers, perhaps, belonged Joseph Adshead, author and member of the Town Council, whose project for a convalescent hospital for Manchester led that " passionate statistician " Florence Nightingale [4] to open the subscription list with a donation of £25; and George Graves, whose revolting description of " Our Sewer Rivers " [5] makes one wonder that human life continued to exist, let alone increase, as it did, in Manchester. Of the different forms of refuse that drained into the rivers the writer remarks :

[1] " On the Defects, with Reference to the Plan of Construction and Ventilation, of most of our Hospitals for the Reception of the Sick and Wounded " (1856); " A Few Additional Suggestions " on the same subject (1858); " On the Need of Additional Hospital Accommodation for Surgical Patients " (1860).

[2] " On the Pavilion Hospital at Chorlton Workhouse," *Trans.*, 1866–7.

[3] " The Insalubrity of the Deep Cornish Mines " (1859); " A Model Warehouse " (1860); " The Application of Ventilation to Dwellings, Schools, and Public Buildings " (1862).

[4] For Miss Nightingale's interest in Statistics see Helen Walker, *History of Statistical Method*, pp. 42–3, 172–4. Adshead's paper was read on December 10, 1860.   [5] Read February 1866.

" The compound thus formed, to be perfectly appreciated, must be seen and smelt. Being, by causes presently to be named, rendered almost stagnant, and the liquids which are poured into it from the manufactories on the banks of the streams being usually warm, it is in the most favourable condition for continued putre-factive fermentation. Every now and then large bubbles rise, which bursting give off noxious gases, and diffuse over the surface solid particles, which, in one of the rivers, the Medlock, at times form a crust so thick that small birds have been seen to walk upon it. The rivers thus contribute their quota to the contamination of the atmosphere."

Graves was an advocate of water-carriage as opposed to those who, largely in the interests of agriculture, desired the continuance of the dry midden. But what he and other reformers wanted was a system of arterial drainage by covered artificial streams.

With the grant of incorporation in 1838 the people of Manchester obtained some of the powers necessary to remedy evils of this kind. Parenthetically, it may be mentioned that it was a member of the Society, Richard Cobden, who led the agitation and moved the resolution for a charter of self-government; that another member, William Neild, acted as Chairman of the Committee for promoting incorporation; and that yet another member, Thomas Potter, became the first Mayor of the borough. Apart from those just mentioned, the list of sixteen new aldermen, moreover, holds names of men like W. R. Callender, John Macvicar, James Murray, John Shuttleworth and Henry Tootall, whose connection with the Society was almost a guarantee that corporate influences would be directed to the work of reform. The common view that the middle class of Manchester was concerned, at this period, solely with the building up of individual fortunes, and remained supine in the face of growing social disharmonies, is possible only to those ignorant alike of the magnitude of the problem and of the steps actually taken to relieve it. The men who won the charter threw themselves into the work of making Manchester a better place to live in and were eager in seeking new powers of control.

In 1846 the first three public parks were opened;[1] in 1851 the Corporation took over the properties of the Manchester and Salford Waterworks Co.; and in the same year an Act was obtained for paving, lighting and cleansing the borough. Two years later other Acts authorised the making and widening of streets; in 1858 powers were obtained for making better provision for the burial of the dead; and other improvement Acts followed. By 1862 some sixty miles of streets had been paved and drained; ninety miles of main sewers and forty-nine miles of cross-sewers had been constructed by the Highways Committee; and new waterworks had been brought into being in the Longdendale Valley.[2]

Impressive as is the record, achievement lagged far behind need. The Town Council was occupied with a score of functions, and until an efficient local civil service had been created, it was inevitable that much of what is now regarded as the proper field of public authority should have been occupied by private enterprise. In 1846 the overburdened Town Council seriously considered the offer of a London Company to carry out a system of drainage and street cleaning and the provision of pure water for domestic use, on a profit-making basis. This concern, which included among its directors Lord Egerton, Thomas Baring, S. J. Loyd, Edwin Chadwick, Nassau Senior and Rowland Hill, offered to take over the waterworks, to provide wash-basins and water-closets for every house (at a cost not exceeding one penny a week for the poorest), to remove household refuse, and to construct and maintain drains without any charge to the town. The revenue was to come from the sale of manure to agriculturists; and, after paying a dividend of 8 per cent., the Company was prepared to hand over half the net profits to the Town Council. [3]

[1] Philip's Park, Peel Park, and Queen's Park.
[2] Kay-Shuttleworth, *Four Periods : Sketch of the Progress of Manchester*, pp. 94-105.
[3] *Manchester Guardian*, March 11, 1846.

This scheme came to nothing. But ten years later a less ambitious plan, of local origin, led to the formation of a company for providing the working classes with baths and laundries. The way had been prepared by an experimental establishment in Miller Street, to which two members of the Society—E. T. Bellhouse and James Dunn—had acted as secretaries, as well as by baths and wash-houses set up by Benjamin Heywood in Miles Platting. For many years following 1856 these elementary comforts of urban life were provided by private enterprise; and it was not until 1877 that the baths and laundries were taken over by the Corporation. During the twenty-one years of its life the Company paid dividends which averaged only 1·6 per cent.; but there is reason to believe that the desire for profit was a lesser motive with the promoters, and that they were not dissatisfied with the results attained.[1]

In spite of public and private efforts directed toward health and cleanliness, about the middle sixties the death-rate of the city showed a disquieting tendency to increase, and in some areas the deaths actually exceeded the births.[2] Such a state gave countenance to those who held that Chadwick and his followers in the struggle against dirt-carried disease had been led to neglect other causes of mortality. Prominent among the critics was Alfred Aspland, a Dukinfield practitioner, who was surgeon to the 4th Cheshire Royal Volunteers, and who became President of the Society in the session 1863-4. A statistician in the true sense of a much-abused word, Aspland resented the way in which preconceived theories, rather than inductions from facts, were being made the basis of legislation; and his defence of the statistical method, set forth in a paper of 1859 on the "Mortality of the Army," is so vigorously phrased as to merit quotation at length.

He is replying to an Edinburgh Reviewer who had

[1] E. T. Bellhouse, "On Baths and Wash-houses for the People," June 1877.
[2] George Graves, "Our Sewer Rivers," p. 28.

remarked that " where men formerly expended their energy on scholastic quibbles they now compile statistics, evincing a mental disease, which may be termed the colliquative diarrhœa of the intellect, indicating a strong appetite and a weak digestion." Aspland is at pains to justify his method. Induction, he insists, is something more than simple inference :

" You must see that you may foresee. You must generalise slowly from particular things to those but one step more general, from those to others of still greater extent, and so on to such as are universal."

But not every student has power to rid his mind of prepossessions, and patience to use the inductive method in its true form :

" The inquirer does not *see* that he may *foresee*, but under a metaphysical nightmare, he *theorises* that he may foresee. He is like the poet, who according to Plautus, when he sets about composing, seeks what is nowhere, and yet finds it. . . . He travels in a dream land, pleasing his fancy with the image of the desert rising in its beauty and order, soon to disappear before the reality of a desolate sand-waste. ' Men see clearly,' says Bacon, ' like owls in the night of their own notions, but in experience, as in the daylight, they wink and are but half-sighted.' It constantly occurs that facts are accepted on authority—the respectability of the narrator leading to the assumption that a rigorous verification is unnecessary. We forget that sagacity is even more necessary than honesty in observation. The Frenchman assured his friend that the earth did turn round the sun, and offered his parole d'honneur as a guarantee; but in the delicate and difficult question of science, paroles d'honneur have a quite inappreciable weight."

Aspland sought to apply Baconian principles to the statistics in the recent *Report on the Sanitary Condition of the Army*, and reached the conclusion that they were mere " numerical incoherencies." A principal officer, he pointed out, in returning a death-rate of 2·25 per cent. for the troops in the Crimea, had declared the position to be " satisfactory." He had failed to add that this was the rate for a *week*, and that if mortality had continued at this rate for a year the Army would have been annihilated.

Aspland's paper makes a close analysis of the causes of disease and death in the forces in time of peace, and gives many examples of official obstruction to the introduction of better conditions.

" Half a century ago," he says, " Lord Melville, from his place in the House of Lords, enunciated his axiom *that the worst men make the best soldiers.* True to the maxim, each successive government did its best to brutalise the unfortunate slave whose necessities had driven him to sell himself body and soul for life, to be shot at, educated in crime, and perhaps flogged to death when he had learned the lesson too well."

" It was generally understood," he concludes, " that during the Duke of Wellington's life-time it was useless to attempt organic reforms in the Army, but it is difficult to understand why so long a period has been allowed to pass over since his death, without any attempt to grapple with giant abuses, to find a remedy for the gathered wrongs that for long years have impaired the efficiency of the Army Surgeon, have made science a mere helpless tool in the hands of arbitrary authority, and which have lowered the moral tone, and prostrated the physical condition of the soldier."

In his inaugural address of 1863 Aspland turned to the problem of civilian deaths, and brought together evidence to show that dirt and putrefaction, though fruitful sources of disease, were not the sole cause :

" Mr. Edwin Chadwick, availing himself of the opportunities which his position as secretary to the Poor Law Board afforded him, addressed inquiries throughout the kingdom to Union officers. Stating his belief, he asked for facts in support of it, and of course obtained them. The consequence was, that what we believe to be a fallacy, took deep root in the popular mind, and prepared the way for an Act of Parliament with a title of highly presumptuous character—' The Nuisances Removal and Diseases Prevention Act.' If my argument is tenable, the second proposition in this title ought to be expunged."

Of like mind was Daniel Noble, whose Presidential Address of 1859 " On Certain Popular Fallacies in the Production of Epidemic Disease " was largely concerned with the visitation of typhus in 1847 and of cholera in 1849. In fighting both, Noble had played a leading part. Of the former he asserted " that its dissemination and virulence were co-extensive, not with the prevalence of nuisances, but rather with the current of Irish immigration so remarkable in that year, and with the degree of communication with the infected strangers "; and the argument that the latter was connected with moisture and filth was rebutted by quotation from the work of a Corresponding member, M. Moreau de Jonnès, who recorded that cholera had raged in Moscow at a time of intense frost, when the supposed causes could not possibly have been in operation.

In a later paper " On Fluctuations in the Death Rate," read in 1863, Noble disposed of several theories connecting the current rate of mortality with the Cotton Famine, setting right those who believed that the stoppage of work had lowered the death rate by diminishing the cotton flue in the atmosphere, and causing the workers to drink less ale, no less than those who thought it had raised the death rate by depressing the standard of life of the workers.

Associated with Aspland and Noble was Henry Wyldebore Rumsey, the celebrated physician of Cheltenham, who had been made a Corresponding member of the Society in 1865. His chief criticism of Chadwick was that he had been responsible for introducing into the administration of Public Health the deterrent policy of the Poor Law. In Rumsey's view the Medical Officer should be, not a mere public informer, but

" in a peculiar sense, the Missionary of Health in his own parish or district—instructing the working classes in personal and domestic hygiene—and practically proving to the helpless and debased, the disheartened and the disaffected, that the State cares for them—a fact of which, until of late, they have seen but little evidence." [1]

[1] Quoted from Rumsey's *Essays in State Medicine* (1856) by B. L. Hutchins, *The Public Health Agitation*, pp. 130–1.

Chadwick was not, however, the only public official subjected to criticism. From its earliest days the Society had kept a watchful eye on the tables of population and deaths. In the first session Robert Hyde Greg had written to the Secretary calling attention to " the extraordinary mortality which occurs every tenth year of human life in the country, commencing with the thirtieth year, and continuing till the nineteenth." Figures were quoted of which the following form a part :

Years.	Number of Deaths.	Years.	Number of Deaths.
29	26,600	69	33,000
30	31,000	70	53,900
31	22,300	71	32,100
39	23,700	79	32,000
40	33,500	80	45,600
41	20,900	81	27,400

" So great an increase regularly occurring," adds Mr. Greg, " during a period of seventy years, without any intermission in the series, cannot be accidental, but must have some fixed and deep-rooted cause, but of such a nature as I cannot trace even in imagination. . . . If any of the Society can explain the cause of this singular series, I shall be happy to hear it."

No reply has been preserved, but surely someone must have pointed out that the cause was just as deep-rooted as the tendency, in the days before registration of births, for those in doubt to state the age of deceased relatives at the nearest round figure.

But even after registration became an accomplished fact there were grave defects in the records; and not the least of the services rendered by Aspland, Noble and Rumsey was to call in question the validity of the annual tables presented by the Registrar-General. In a note appended to his paper on " The Mortality of the Army " Aspland says :

" Until it is generally known that the classification of diseases in the Registrar-General's Reports is absolutely worthless—that the elaborate tables, believed in and quoted in support of arguments by men of science over the whole civilised world—forming the materials of cram for members of Parliament who devote themselves to Sanitary Reform—are about as trustworthy as historical documents as the details of Moll Flanders' income and expenditure, or Robinson Crusoe's adventures—constant and increasing injury must accrue to our national interests."

And in his inaugural address of 1863 he writes of the population tables as follows :

" Cobbett was fond of extracting his instances of bad grammar from Royal speeches; and, following his example, we may cull from Government Statistics the most remarkable violations of the Baconian code.   Theory-begotten facts are often collected with the most reckless carelessness; series of them are grouped which allow of no comparison, and inferences are drawn with a prodigal disregard of logic.   The broad arrow must be placed on them, and a rigorous analysis instituted before they can be received as true. . . .   Our population returns will bear a comparison with the best statistics of any country in Europe, as far as numbers, sex and perhaps age are concerned; but when we attempt to arrive at other social facts, such as employment and religious belief, there is an obvious breakdown.   Porter tells us that the specification of employments in 1831 indicated 5,030 coachbuilders, and only one coach-spring maker; the whole kingdom gave employment to only three coffin makers, each of whom would have to provide 300 coffins daily throughout the year—and so on."

It was probably Dr. Rumsey's paper " On the Value of Life Tables as Evidence of Sanitary Conditions," read in November 1866, that led the Society to appoint a Committee to inquire into the defects in the system of registration of deaths and to send a memorial on the subject to the Home Office a few months later.   The report and memorial pointed out that in 17 per cent. of all recorded cases of death the cause was uncertified : they urged that notification should be made compulsory ; that the local officers should be properly trained for their duties ; and that they should be adequately paid so as to be able to withstand the pressure of vested interests.

In 1868, largely as the result of the advocacy of David Chadwick (the Salford Borough Treasurer),

Manchester acquired the services of a Medical Officer
of Health.   That the same critical approach was
necessary to the annual reports of this official was
demonstrated a few years later.   In the report for
1874 the Medical Officer had given the death rate for
an Ardwick enumeration district as 3·3 per thousand,
and that for the neighbouring London Road district
at no less a figure than 70 per thousand, on the
average of the years 1861–70.   It was left to a member
of the Society to explain such a disparity.   In a paper
read in 1875 Robert Martin pointed out that the population figures on which the rates were based had been
taken from the Census of 1871.   But in the one district
where, during the greater part of the decade, the population had been small, many new dwellings had been
erected shortly before the Census; thus "owing to the
previous smallness of the population, the deaths were
very few, and when divided into the large population of
1871, gave necessarily a very small death rate."   In
the other area, just before the Census enumeration, some
600 houses had been pulled down by the Midland
Railway Company.   "Hence the annual average number
of deaths during the previous ten years, being divided
among a population lessened by at least one-third of the
number among which the deaths had occurred, gave a
proportionally increased and excessive death-rate."[1]

In opposition to the works of the Registrar-General,
and, indeed, of all centrally-appointed officials, the
writers so far mentioned were far exceeded by Edward
Herford, to whom reference will be made in a
later chapter.   In Herford's view the supreme danger
was that of the growth of bureaucracy.   "To prevent
the people of a place from managing their own
affairs," he says, "is one of the principal resources of
arbitrary power on the one hand and of communistic
democracy on the other."   The methods employed
were first, "the vesting in the Secretary of State the
power to decide upon an infinite variety of matters

[1] "Sanitary Progress and its Obstacles in Manchester," April 1875.

which are better decided upon the spot." Secondly, the setting up in London of numerous boards like the Ecclesiastical Commission, the Poor Law Board, the Board of Health, the Privy Council Committee on Education, and "that most devastating body, the Charity Commission, which is rapidly depriving the industrious and hard-working people of England of the educational institutions which belong to them." Thirdly, the creation of "a whole army of Factory, Poor Law, Burial Board, School, Sanitary and other Inspectors, irresponsible to the people, practically irresponsible to Parliament, who exercise throughout the length and breadth of the land that paternal authority which men despise when exercised by legitimate governments abroad, and which is, amongst us, gradually but surely sapping local intelligence and public spirit, by taking away the means and occasion for their frequent and legitimate exercise." And, finally, the placing of the management of county police, prisons and lunatic asylums in the hands of "a certain number of gentlemen in each county whose names happen to be inscribed, through influences never precisely known to the public, upon a formidable piece of parchment called a 'Commission of the Peace,' signed by one of the officers of State." [1]

In defending his own ancient office of Coroner against the alleged invasion of central government, Herford was led to adverse comment on the statement of the Registrar-General that "the fact of death being sudden was no ground for the holding of an inquest." "The Registrar-General," declared Herford, "subordinates the protection of human life to the mere collection of statistics and . . . it is of no consequence whether they are correct or not, so long as they are *precisely expressed* in Latin or English terms, and reducible into 'quarterly tables of the causes of death.' " [2] The result was an exchange of letters in some of which Herford expressed

[1] Edward Herford, "On the Principles and Practice of Municipal Institutions in England," January 1865.
[2] "On Alleged Defects in the Office of Coroner," January 1877.

his views with what is sometimes described as a typically Manchester directness of phrase. But that a man of spirit was hidden behind the official mask of the Registrar-General is indicated by a letter [1] sent in reply to one addressed to him, at Herford's request, by the Secretary of the Northern Coroner's Committee. It reads :

> *General Registry Office,*
> *Somerset House.*
>
> *Jan. 24th, 1877.*
>
> SIR,
>
> Another person has commenced writing to me from Manchester stating that what he says is dictated by you.
>
> The opinions you think it right to express respecting me and Civil Registration generally are not very flattering; but to my mind I assure you they are held in the same estimation as if they were highly complimentary.
>
> If it is a comfort and satisfaction to you thus frequently to give vent to your excited feelings upon this subject, don't hesitate to write me here often—once a week, if you like.
>
> I know what to do with this lengthened correspondence; there is a large pigeon hole in this office appropriated to it, and it is not yet full.
>
> Your faithful servant,
>
> GEORGE GRAHAM,
> *Registrar-General.*
>
> THE CORONER,
> MANCHESTER.

---

[1] Printed as Appendix to Herford's paper, *Trans.*, 1876–7, p. 66.

CHAPTER V

THE STRUGGLE FOR PUBLIC EDUCATION

CONTROVERSIES arising out of the methods of raising the standard of public health were not the only ones to engage the minds of members during these years. The problem of physical destitution, and the even more intractable one of educational destitution were ever present. In December 1852, before the beginning of the *Transactions*, a new interest had been kindled by a paper on " The Condition and Education of Poor Children in English and German Towns," read by Joseph Kay, a younger brother of James Kay-Shuttleworth. Kay, who was later to become Judge of the Salford Hundred Court of Record, was at this time a barrister in London, and a Corresponding member of the Society. Extensive foreign travel had given him an intimate knowledge of the life of foreign cities ; and on English conditions his paper gives numerous citations from the *Report on Criminal and Destitute Juveniles* (1852), the *Report on the Criminal Law* (1847), and the speeches of Lord Ashley.

Remarking that the provincial city was a new phenomenon that had grown up without proper organisation for self-government, Kay called attention to the degraded condition of the juvenile population as one of its dominant characteristics. Of this " offspring of our neglect " he quotes a writer [1] as follows :

" The City Arab has, in truth, all the vices, and some of the virtues of the savage; he is indolent, averse from any steady or settled employment, averse from restraint of any kind. On the other hand, he is patient of hunger, thirst and cold; and as to

[1] M. D. Hill, the Recorder of Birmingham.

dirt, he rather delights in it than otherwise; and he would much rather be permitted to roam about at large, even suffering at times great privations, than he would be at school, or at work, under the restraints which belong to civilised society.

" Their code is, in general, that he is the best boy or lad, who can obtain subsistence, or satisfy the wants of life with the least labour—by begging or stealing—or who shows the greatest dexterity in accomplishing his object, and the greatest wariness in escaping the penalties of justice; and lastly, the greatest powers of endurance and defiance, when he comes under the lash of the law.

" The abodes of such of these ' City Arabs ' as have any abodes at all except dry arches, doorsteps or the hedges, are as miserable as can be imagined. They sleep in dirty, unwholesome, ill-drained tenements—in rooms too small for the separation of the sexes and for the purposes of decency. As many as forty and fifty ' Arabs ' sometimes sleep in one room, boys and girls promiscuously. At fifteen or sixteen years of age the male ' Arab ' is mated—*but not with a wife.* They indulge in intoxicating liquors, are afflicted with unmentionable and degrading diseases, and are far more vicious in their conduct and filthy in their persons and their language than full-grown men and women of their own class. They seem to have a well-defined organisation among them, or something nearly akin to it. A certain class of ' City Arabs ' do nothing but steal provisions from shop doors and sell them for one tenth of their value, or less, to the infamous keepers of the abominable lodging-houses which they frequent; a second class pick men's pockets and never touch a woman's; a third devote themselves exclusively to the picking of women's pockets, and refrain from meddling with those of men; while a fourth do nothing but ' draw the dampers,' *i.e.* steal from shop tills. In London there are regular gangs, each of which is commanded by a leader or ' Captain '. . . ."

The paper gives much information on juvenile crime, on common lodging-houses, and on the Singing Rooms and Penny Theatres where the town child found unwholesome recreation and instruction in new forms of vice. The remedy, in Kay's opinion, was to establish " refuges and playgrounds for the worst class of our town children, and to send them thither every day "; he urged that each municipality should be given power to levy a rate to pay the school pence and find comfortable clothing for indigent children, and that every parent in receipt of outdoor relief should be compelled to send his children daily to school.

The comparison of child life in English with that in German and Swiss towns was far from soothing to British pride. But that the evils were due to lack of schooling, and not to industrialism, was emphasised in a paper of January 1856, " On Juvenile Criminals, Reformatories and the Means of Rendering the Perishing and Dangerous Classes Serviceable to the State." The author, Joseph Adshead, sought to demonstrate by quotation from Plint's *Crime in England* " that it is *not the manufacturing system*, and especially *the factory system*, that increases juvenile crime. Lancashire and the West Riding of York represent that system, and both show *a diminishing ratio of juvenile offences*."

" The facts are now patent which men, not blinded by prejudice, and not having their mental vision intercepted by foregone conclusions, have for some time strongly surmised, viz. that the morality of the manufacturing population ranks above the agricultural; and it must be borne in special remembrance that in this comparison no allowance is made for the incidence on crime of the incessant immigration of the worst classes of the Irish population into the manufacturing districts, nor for the amount of crime committed in those districts by the predatory classes, who find plunder and refuge there, but have no affinity with the indigenous and operative classes. If the incidence of these two disturbing causes could be estimated, little doubt exists that the ratio of crime in the manufacturing districts would exhibit a far more favourable character."

Those who took an optimistic view of the results of industrialisation in the area could find some support from the researches of David Chadwick, afterwards M.P. for Macclesfield, who joined the Society in 1858–9, became Secretary in 1860, and served as President from 1865 to 1867. A first paper of 1861,[1] it is true, gives an unfavourable impression of the standard of health in the district; for Chadwick's comparative tables for the year

[1] " On the Best Means of Obtaining and Recording the Vital Statistics of Towns," February 1861,

1858 show Manchester and Salford heading the list of large towns with death rates respectively of 34·09 and 34·11, against a rate of only 27·14 for London.   But in the same year he presented to the Society a mass of statistics [1] relating to the two towns, which show evidence of marked social advance.   Between 1841 and 1860 there had come about a decrease in the number of public-houses (though that of beer-houses and brothels, it must be admitted, had grown).   During the same period the circulation of local newspapers had expanded nearly twenty-fold.   Between 1839 and 1859 the wages of skilled workers in the cotton industry had increased by 10–25 per cent.[2]   And an inquiry into the cost of living of a family of five persons showed that the same quantities of food, fuel and clothing which in 1839–40 would have cost 24s. 9d., could have been bought in 1859–60 for 20s. 6d.—a fall attributed by Chadwick to the repeal of the Corn Laws and the reduction of the duties on tea, coffee, sugar and soap.

But that progress in the community could exist along with acute poverty in some of its parts was amply demonstrated by a series of social surveys made by the Society a few years later.   In March 1864 the Executive Committee made a grant of £20 to defray the expenses of an inquiry into the condition of a district in the Deansgate and Peter Street area,[3] where a visitation was made of 713 inhabited houses and sixty-eight inhabited cellars. Here no fewer than 297 families (28 per cent. of the whole) were found living in single rooms ; 180 of the houses had no back-yards, and where such existed they were commonly used as pigsties.   Poverty was sometimes extreme.   " In one family they never have any

[1] " On the Social and Educational Statistics of Manchester and Salford," November 1861.

[2] In March 1860 David Chadwick presented to the London Statistical Society an important paper on " The Rate of Wages in 200 Trades and Branches of Labour in Manchester and Salford and the Manufacturing District of Lancashire, during twenty years, from 1839 to 1859."

[3] Report, session 1863–4.   The results of the inquiry were printed in the *Transactions*, 1864–5.

meat, their chief food being bread and tea. Another family of four persons, whose income is 4s., and rent 1s. 9d., have for five months had only one meal a day; and another of three persons, where the husband and wife both work, and earn between them 5s. a week, and pay 1s. rent, have also but one meal a day." It was, let it be remembered, the period of the Cotton Famine; and, in spite of the fact that other inquiries suggested that this had not been responsible for much actual destitution, it would hardly be safe to consider such conditions as normal.[1]

The Deansgate inquiry was followed immediately by one into a district in Ancoats, covering 607 houses, of which sixty-eight had cellar dwellings let off as tenements. Of the families 19 per cent. occupied one room each; and 65 per cent. of the houses had no through passage and no back yard. " One man keeps a large bull-dog for fighting purposes. Another man keeps a pony and a pig in the scullery, and also rabbits and dogs about the house. In another case the kitchen was found to be a stable for a donkey, and on visiting one of the courts in the district a second time, it was found that the police had been since the first visit, and compelled the inhabitants to remove no less than five donkeys from their houses." Of 700 children between the ages of three and twelve, 310 were either at day school or at work; but only three children from the whole district attended night school. The average family income, which in the Deansgate district had been found to be 16s. 11d., was in Ancoats 18s. 11d.[2]

Four years later, in April 1868, T. R. Wilkinson supplemented the Deansgate inquiry by another into conditions at Gaythorn and Knott Mill, near by, the cost

[1] In the session 1862-3, the Society spent two of its meetings in considering the problems of relief of distress arising from the Cotton Famine, and another in listening to the Rev. Alexander Munro's somewhat pompous account of " Our Unemployed Females, and What may Best be Done for Them " (March 1863).

[2] Transactions, November 1865.

of which was met by his senior officer in the Manchester and Salford Bank, William Langton. Of 628 families, over a quarter of which were Irish, about a fifth occupied one room each; 35 per cent. of the children of school age had never been to a day school; 47 per cent. of the adults could not read; and 65 per cent. were unable to write.[1]

Such revelations gave support to those members who, for more than a generation, had been urging on the Government the need for public education. It has already been suggested that the reports of the early days of the Society had been largely responsible for the more active intervention of the State and the setting up of the Committee of Council. Locally, their firstfruit had been the creation, in 1837, by such men as Richard Cobden, James Heywood and Mark Philips, of a branch of the National Education Society; and in the same year the Manchester Society for Promoting National Education was brought into being. This body, in which the leading spirits were men like Cobden, Langton, Benjamin Heywood, Edward Herford and R. H. Greg, advocated State aid and unsectarian religious education. It was responsible for setting up three schools in the town, financed partly by the fees of scholars, but largely by grants from the Society.[2] During the period of the anti-Corn Law agitation the activities declined. But in 1847 some of its supporters, including such members of the Statistical Society as John Watts, Dr. McKerrow and John Mills, formed the Lancashire Public School Association, which aimed at non-sectarian education maintained by local rates and controlled by locally-elected committees.[3] Out of this, in turn, sprang the National Public School

[1] *Transactions*, April 1868.
[2] S. L. Maltby, *Manchester and the Movement for National Elementary Education*, pp. 49–54, 153; F. Smith, *Life of Sir James Kay-Shuttleworth*, pp. 75–6.
[3] Cobden was a Vice-President, and among other members of the Statistical Society who served on the Committee were W. R. Callender, S. D. Darbyshire, H. R. Forrest, E. R. Langworthy, Samuel Robinson and S. A. Steinthal.

Association, the promoters of which included Cobden, Benjamin Heywood and Hugh Mason, with its head-quarters in Manchester.

To many, however, the secularist or non-sectarian solution was unacceptable. In 1844, the local clergy had formed the Manchester Church Education Society, to which the Rev. Charles Richson (President of the Statistical Society 1857–9) acted as Secretary. In 1851 Canon Richson put forward, with the approval of Kay-Shuttleworth, a project for a Bill to enable Manchester and Salford to create a system of free education maintained out of local rates, but conducted by the religious bodies, which would have the right to include doctrinal instruction in the curriculum. The Manchester and Salford Committee on Education, which was set up to further the plan, included among its members Thomas Bazley, W. R. Callender, Oliver Heywood and E. R. Langworthy. But the Town Council was opposed to a scheme that would put the cost and responsibility of public education on the local authority, and the Bill failed to pass.[1]

If no immediate solution was to be looked for from Parliament, those eager for extension of education could do something through voluntary bodies. As the result of a series of eloquent letters to the *Manchester Guardian*, written by Edward Brotherton (a member of the Statistical Society), the Manchester and Salford Education Aid Society was formed in 1864. Its objects were to pay part of the school fees of poor children and, if necessary, to set up free schools ; and its founders included members of our Society of such diverse views as Richard Copley Christie, J. A. Bremner, Samuel Robinson and John Watts. A statistical inquiry made by this body in the New Cross and St. Michael's wards showed that " half the youthful population of the working class is unable to write, and about one-fourth is unable to read " ; and a house-to-house visitation conducted by T. R. Wilkinson for the Statistical Society in 1867 revealed a similar state

[1] Maltby, *op. cit.*, Ch. VII.

of illiteracy.   Of 733 children of school age, 258, or
35 per cent., had never been to a day school; and of the
adult population of the area only 53 per cent. could read,
and only 35 per cent. could write.   Comparison with
the investigations made in neighbouring areas in 1851
suggested that, in spite of a generation of effort, no
advance had been made in day-school attendance, while
an actually smaller proportion of the children were
attending Sunday Schools than at the earlier date.

Within two years of its formation the Manchester
and Salford Education Aid Society discovered the sur-
prising fact that " in many instances it is impossible to
persuade the parents to accept the gift of education."
Another Manchester Education Bill prepared by the
Committee was introduced into Parliament in April
1867.   It proposed that, by a vote of the majority of
the rate-payers, schools might be built and grants made
to existing schools at which the fees were not more than
ninepence a week.[1]   But to many it appeared a half-
hearted measure.   Members of the Statistical Society,
like Thomas Ashton, the Rev. H. E. Dowson, Elijah
Helm, Alderman Rumsey and the Rev. S. A. Steinthal,
preferred to give support to the National Education
League, which, founded in Birmingham in 1869, aimed
at an entirely new system of free, compulsory, unsectarian
instruction.   Others followed the new Bishop, James
Fraser, in supporting the National Education Union,
which sought to maintain the traditional religious basis
with denominational schools.   It would be out of place
to attempt to describe the struggles that followed and the
process of agitation in Parliament and outside.   Suffice
it to say that the Act finally passed under Gladstone's
Ministry was a compromise between the measures
proposed by these warring bodies.

It is impossible to appraise precisely the part played
by Manchester men in making possible the Education
Act of 1870.   That it was by no means small was
evidenced by the fact that the town was the headquarters

[1] Maltby, *op. cit.*, p. 107.

of so many of the propagandist bodies; and we have the word of that high authority, Sir Michael Sadler, that " the work of the educational reformers in Manchester between 1840 and 1865, though it seemed to be a failure, was in fact the foundation on which the new system of English public elementary education was based." [1]

Not the least influential of the reformers were members of the Statistical Society, and in the Society's rooms religionist and secularist, Conservative and Liberal, could meet, not to fight, but to survey the ground they held in common. Perhaps the most doughty champion of popular education among our members was John Watts, the son of a Coventry ribbon weaver, who had come to Manchester in 1840 as a communist orator. The fact that this agnostic could work in close association with Canon Richson for the Manchester Education Bill was, no doubt, due to the large-mindedness of both; but is it too much to hazard the guess that the co-operation was facilitated by a common fellowship in the Statistical Society?

It was with extreme reluctance that many members came to support compulsion. When, in 1865, John Roberton read his paper " On the Duty of England to Provide a Gratuitous Compulsory Education for the Children of her Poorer Classes " he would go only half way : " I do not," he said, " advocate *direct* compulsion —the forcing of parents to send their children by the infliction of legal penalties—but that *indirect* compulsion which operates on the selfish feelings ; I mean the withholding of outdoor poor relief from such as neglect to avail themselves of what the law gratuitously provides for their benefit." And in the following year Samuel Robinson [2] declared that though compulsion was impracticable, an approach to it might be obtained by an extension of the Factory Acts, and insistence that " wages and school must go together and that attendance at the

[1] " The Story of Education in Manchester " in *The Soul of Manchester* (ed. by W. H. Brindley), p. 51.
[2] " On the Education of the Lower Classes," March 1866.

one must be a condition of receiving the other." But when, in his Presidential Address three years later, Stanley Jevons [1] declared, " Compulsory attendance at school we must have," there were probably no dissentients. His plea that some member should investigate the most efficient way of carrying out the future law called forth two papers : one from the veteran Samuel Robinson,[2] urging the setting up of a Ministry of Public Education, and another from John Bremner,[3] which laid down principles not very different from those that were to find embodiment in Forster's Act.

[1] " On the Work of the Society in Connection with the Questions of the Day," November 1869.

[2] " On Combined Religious and Secular Instruction," December 1869.

[3] " On the Principles of Compulsion in Primary Education," January 1870.

CHAPTER VI

INDUSTRIAL FLUCTUATIONS AND BANKING POLICY

I

THE preceding chapters have been concerned mainly with the contributions of Manchester statisticians to social reform. During the same period members of the Society did much to enlarge the bounds of economic thought; and in the sphere of banking and currency theory, in particular, constructive work of a high order was presented in the Society's rooms during the fifties, sixties, and early seventies of last century. The series of papers began during the financial crisis of 1857 with one in which William Langton [1] presented tables based on the returns of the Bank of England from 1844 to 1857. The fundamental idea of Langton seems to be that of the existence of a " fund of credit," a fund that was dealt in by bankers and Discount Houses, as well as by the State.

" The Banker sells his own credit when he takes in a deposit; he buys that of other people when he employs that deposit in discounting bills, or makes a lodgment of cash with an agent or bill broker. He may also buy the credit of the State by investing in Stock, or Exchequer Bills. . . . The State itself in this country is, however, the most gigantic trader in credit ever known in the history of the world, and enjoys a confidence of the public little less than miraculous. She has actually sold so much of her own credit, as has brought into her hands above eight hundred millions of the accumulated wealth of the country, and she has literally nothing to show for it."

Of this credit sold by the State fourteen and a half

[1] " Observations on a Table showing the Balance of Account between the Mercantile Public and the Bank of England," December 1857.

millions had been used, under the Bank Charter Act of
1844, as the basis for the issue of a corresponding
amount of paper money—a mistake in Langton's view,
" since it seems likely to act as an incentive to the inflation of credit and to reckless speculation."

" If," he says, " the recent financial embarrassment of the country
has been brought about by an undue extension of foreign commerce,
which has more than exhausted the floating capital of the country,
there must be some fund of credit upon which it has impinged in
the process.   Is not the public credit of the country always staked
to supply such a fund of expansion ? and is it not more than probable
that this circumstance strongly promotes among us the spirit to
over-trade ? Is not this expansive power supplied by the fourteen
and a half millions of the bank-note circulation, which has no
basis upon bullion; resting, therefore, not upon the Capital, but
on the Credit of the country ? "

His paper concludes, therefore, with the inquiry
" whether the existence of a fund of credit, forming by
law a portion of the basis of the circulation, does not
operate with a vicious impulse on the community, almost
uncontrollable by any action emanating from the Bank
Parlour."

In his opposition to the fiduciary issue, and his belief
that its abolition would remove booms and panics,
Langton showed himself to belong to the right wing of
the Currency School.   But the interest of his paper lies
less in his views than in the statistics he presented.
Setting down for each week the difference between the
amount of Other Securities and Other Deposits, he
argued that " as one or the other of these two items is
in excess, we discover whether the mercantile community are in a condition of ease, with unemployed
funds at call, or whether their necessities require them
to lean for assistance on the Bank of England,—and
in what degree."   To-day the problem would be expressed in terms of Money Market rates and the extent
to which bill brokers were having recourse to the Bank.
But it is unnecessary to discuss here either the ways in
which the differences between Other Deposits and Other

Securities might vary, or the appropriateness of Langton's index. The importance of his work lies in the revelation of three main tendencies :

First, " an almost invariable increase in the demands of the public upon the Bank from the second week in each quarter up to the first week in the following one. This is accounted for by the gradual absorption of the means of the public through the collection of the revenue, and the release of these funds by the payment of the dividends."

Secondly, a seasonal fluctuation to be " traced in the magnitude of the operations of the third and fourth quarters, and the almost invariable lull in the second quarter of each year ; the third quarter being generally marked by rapid increase in the demand for accommodation at the Bank."

Thirdly, " Another wave, which appears to have a decennial period, and in the generation of which moral causes have no doubt an important share."

It was this last of the three fluctuations that was to engage so much of the best energy of the Society during the coming years. Langton was by no means the first to observe the existence of the trade cycle : it had been noticed by a journalist, John Wade, in 1833 ; Samuel Jones Loyd (afterwards Lord Overstone) had, as early as 1837, attempted to describe its successive stages ; and Hyde Clarke had argued that there must be some physical cause for the periodical fluctuations.[1] But we have the word of Jevons [2] that William Langton " independently remarked the existence of a decennial cycle " ; and, if for no other reason, his paper deserves to be remembered as the first expression of the idea (made familiar to-day by D. H. Robertson) that the trade cycle may, perhaps, be the necessary price of economic progress.

[1] Wesley Mitchell, *Business Cycles*, pp. 7–11.
[2] Jevons, *Investigations in Currency and Finance*, p. 223.

" Whether—allowing that the equalisation of wealth over the face of the earth is in the end a great benefit—this object," asks Langton, " be not more rapidly accomplished by such spasmodic action, than by the steady though slow progress of a cautious trade. While there are naked people to be clothed, hungry to be fed, and waste places to be cultivated, there is great scope for the extension of commerce. The consuming powers of many foreign markets have only been ascertained after immense sacrifices on the part of the speculators who first opened them. Had it depended on our cautious capitalists, the network of railways which covers the land would not yet have been created."

Langton clearly belonged to what would now be termed the monetary school of trade-cycle theorists, as did also T. H. Williams, who, on the same evening of 1857, read a paper entitled " Observations on Money, Credit and Panics." But the lines of demarcation between different bodies of thought were less sharply drawn than now, and it would be possible for those who hold that the monetary phenomena of the cycle reflect (or produce) underlying changes in the structure of production to claim Williams as a precursor.

" One common mode in which a too easy condition of credit leads to a derangement," he wrote, " is that of an excessive conversion of floating into fixed capital. There must be a due proportion between these two classes of capital in order that their joint efficiency may be fully realised. It is obviously worse than profitless to divert so much labour from the production of goods to the making of railways, or from the growing of raw materials to the making of machines, as that we have not goods enough to employ the former, nor raw materials enough to keep the latter profitably at work. When this disproportion takes place in such vast undertakings as railways, a proportionate monetary derangement is the consequence."

Six years later, in his pamphlet on *A Serious Fall in the Value of Gold*, Jevons wrote:[1]

" That great commercial fluctuations, completing their course in ten years, diversify the progress of trade, is familiar to all who attend to mercantile matters. The remote cause of these commercial tides has not been so well ascertained. It seems to lie

[1] *Investigations*, p. 28.

in the *varying proportions which the capital devoted to permanent and remote investment bears to that which is but temporarily invested soon to reproduce itself*."

It is highly probable that Jevons had seen Williams' paper : but, in any case, unless it can be shown that he had the idea from some earlier writer, we may claim that an important strand in the modern theory of business cycles was originated by a member of the Society at this early date.

The passage cited, it is true, does not set beyond doubt whether Williams regarded the monetary factor as cause or effect of economic disequilibrium. But at least he had no sympathy with the view, common to-day, that all that is necessary for the maintenance of prosperity is to hold up the general level of prices.

" Many persons," he says, " seeing that, in a crisis, money and credit become immensely contracted, are indeed anxious for some intervention which shall prevent such contraction, with its attendant fall of prices. They do not see that the inflation of prices constitutes a state of derangement which can be corrected only by a collapse of credit and of prices."

His own remedies were, first, greater publicity on the part of the banks—weekly returns, like those of the Bank of England, from all the private and joint-stock banks : secondly, the abolition of the fiduciary issue and the assumption of the issue of notes, by " a State Issue Office, under a manager appointed for life by the Cabinet, but removable by the House of Commons ; holding always in his vaults an amount of gold equal to that of the ' promises to pay ' in the hands of the public." He cherished no illusions, indeed, that such a system would banish over-trading ; but urged that " if Parliament were to put an end to its own evil example of authorising one huge structure of mere paper, resting upon a basis of other paper, it might then tell the people that if they will still build upon that sort of foundation, in the shape of accommodation bills, or imprudent ledger credits, they must bear the unmitigated consequences." Education by sad experience was the only remedy. " If bankers, traders, and merchants were left to help one another through the next self-inflicted crisis, they would come out of it with wiser—though perhaps greyer—heads."

It was no accident that the Society should have turned its attention to these questions in 1857, when the depression following the collapse was at its worst; and it was no accident that the next contribution to the subject should have been made in the year following the succeeding crisis of 1866. This was the work of John Mills, of whom Jevons [1] remarks that he had "almost made this subject his own." Mills, who was born at Ashton-under-Lyne in 1821, had entered the service of the Manchester and Liverpool District Bank at the age of sixteen. After serving the Bank at Ashton and Rochdale, he became a branch manager at Nantwich in 1852, and twelve years later moved to Bowdon, on his appointment as General Manager of the Alliance Bank, a position he held till he joined the directorate of the Lancashire and Yorkshire Bank in 1889. He was a man of literary tastes, and his wife has left a biography which shows the close personal intimacy of Mills with some of the leading figures in Victorian literature. [2]   In 1866 he read before the economics section of the National Social Science meeting a paper on " The Bank Charter Act and the Late Panic," and this was followed in the next year by his important paper to the Statistical Society " On Credit Cycles and the Origin of Commercial Panics."

Mills gives a valuable synopsis of the six commercial panics of the century (those of 1815, 1825, 1835–9, 1847, 1857, and 1866) and describes, in each case, the special features and special effects. Arguing that the common attribution of crises to over-trading was insufficient explanation, since over-trading is not an

---

[1] *Investigations*, p. 224.
[2] *From Tinder-Box to the " Larger Light."* Incidentally John Mills was the uncle of two distinguished journalists, John Saxon Mills and William Haslam Mills.

ultimate fact, the writer suggests that "the subject of commercial fluctuation will acquire a new dignity if it be found striking its roots far below the level of its physical particulars, and proving itself cognate with the sciences of the mind." Two facts he takes as established : first the *periodicity* of crises, and second " that the instances are already too numerous, regular, and persistent, to allow any foothold for a theory of fortuitous coincidence." The fact that crises have occurred under a régime of inconvertible currency, under that of free issues of convertible paper, and under that of regulated issues on a gold basis, suggests that the causes do not lie with the currency system, and leads to the hypothesis that " the malady of commercial crisis is not, in essence, a matter of the *purse* but of the mind." After these preliminary observations, Mills lays down the thesis that "the decades interposed between the great commercial crises are normal cycles of development of Credit under certain existing conditions ; that during each of these decades commercial credit runs through the mutations of a life, having its infancy, growth to maturity, diseased overgrowth, and death by collapse ; and that each cycle is composed of well-marked normal stages, corresponding to these ideas in nature and succession." It is this conception of a normal cycle that was new ; and the division into four phases of Speculation, Panic, Post-Panic, and Revival, has been followed by later writers, like Wesley Mitchell, under the different nomenclature of Prosperity, Crisis (or Recession), Depression, and Revival.[1]

According to Mills, " Panic is the destruction, in the mind, of a bundle of beliefs." A mass of paper documents, the outward expression of this belief, has been destroyed, and its place has to be taken by currency. " The Panic period is therefore marked by great scarcity of mobile capital ; because though not less in quantity

[1] Wesley Mitchell, *op. cit.*, pp. 378, 387. Clement Juglar had in 1860 distinguished three stages—prosperity, crisis, and liquidation. *Ibid.*, p. 452.

than before, it is drafted off into a thousand unusual
channels to perform the functions commonly exercised
by Credit."

The Post-Panic is characterised by a falling off in
the demand for loans, and an accumulation of resources
in the Banks. This plethora of resources at a low rate
of interest does not, however, lead to a speedy revival,
for " economy, enforced on great numbers of people by
losses from failures and from depreciated investments,
restricts their purchasing power ; and a diminished
wages-fund does the same thing in relation to the working classes. Profits are kept down to the stunted proportions of demand." With the fall in prices, the
exchanges turn in a favourable direction, and " the tide
of money-Capital flows towards this country, and helps
to swell the abundance already resulting from the
internal causes before specified."

After two or three years this phase merges into that
of Revival, in which new firms come into being, controlled by men " to whom the grim story of past panics,
and of the nemesis of over-speculation, is a mere myth,
or at most a matter of hearsay tradition." For a time
profit-making is healthy, but later " the actual incre-
ment of Capital from profits begins to overflow the
usual channels of investment ; and in seeking for new
channels, the *habit* of contemplating a high scale of
profits makes men look over old-fashioned modes of
investment to others which promise better things."

Thus the period of Recovery passes into that of
Speculation, and there occurs an expansion of credit out
of proportion to the supplies of loanable capital. " Credit
and speculation act upon each other as reciprocal stimu-
lants. Inflated Credit, by elevating prices and profits,
tempts to further speculation ; and speculation can only
be carried on by multiplying instruments of Credit." . . .
" There is a morbid excess of belief, an *hypertrophy* of
belief, induced by an excess of nourishment to that
faculty of the mind." The result is the rise of prices
which breaks down the purchasing power of the market

and leads to a collapse. As the price of commodities falls so also does that of those securities which represent public works, like railways. "These securities are always largely pledged, and the institutions holding them are at such times driven to realise at current values in exchange. This crucial test throws a new light upon the dangerous rapidity with which Capital has been fixed in these works, and reveals how far even Credit is committed to further works of postponed productiveness." The conclusion of it all is that the cycle arises from " the tendency of the faculty of credit to grow." " Credit, then, we know to be a thing of growth through normal and predictable stages; and, under existing conditions, it is deciduous at intervals of about ten years." The argument is next advanced that there must be preserved in a condition of healthy trade, an equilibrium between Credit and Capital. " The ratio of the growth of Credit prescribes the ratio of the demand for Capital, and therefore, the rate of its hire." A rise in the rate of interest has a dual effect. " On the one hand its attractive force upon Capital replenishes the reserves needful to sustain Credit, when the competition for loans has increased : on the other, by bearing more or less heavily on the sensitive surface of Profit, it applies an effective brake to the dangerous velocity with which a too facile Credit would multiply transactions. In both ways it tends to preserve that natural and (to a country like this, which besides trading so closely up to its own means, is a centre for the financial operations of the world) that vitally important equipoise between the growth of bill-making Credit and the supply of Capital from accumulated profits and savings." But during the Speculative stage equilibrium is upset. The demand for credit for permanent investment abroad and for works of postponed productiveness at home is intense ; but raising the rate of interest fails to attract capital either from home or abroad in sufficient quantities, and the inverted pyramid of Credit collapses.

To the question as to whether Credit must always

" grow rank and rotten, and collapse in a spasm of terror," Mills replies that it may be fairly hoped that credit cycles can be indefinitely lengthened and their evils mitigated.[1]   But this can come only by the education of business men.   " It is the liability to an *ignorant* speculative excitement, and a willingness to take *immoral* risks, which ultimately put the growth of Credit beyond the control of the price of loan Capital.   Diminish these and the cycle may then expand beyond its customary decade."   Asserting that " the schoolmaster, rather than the legislator, is the magician who is to steady our rates of discount, and save Lombard Street from its decennial fits of terror," Mills urged that Manchester was sounder in matters of monetary science than most other commercial communities—the Birmingham School had found little support here—and added that the institution of the Cobden Chair of Political Economy at Owens College placed on her the obligation to diffuse " the special kind of culture required to diminish the disasters we are met to discuss." [2]

Modern writers, like Wesley Mitchell, have put John Mills' essay, along with Professor Pigou's great work on *Industrial Fluctuations*, into the pigeon-hole they have labelled " Psychological Theories."   They might, however, with equal justice, have put it into another occupied by the works of Mr. Hawtrey, or into yet a third along with the writings of Mr. Keynes.   The truth is that,

[1] Cf. Wesley Mitchell, *Business Cycles*, p. 458.   " There is evidence that business cycles keep changing character as economic organisation develops.   The most violent manifestations are brought under control. Panics subside into crises and crises into recessions."

[2] This opinion of Manchester's soundness was not shared ·by every member.   Edward Herford began his address " On Facts and Fictions of the Currency " (June 1875) as follows :   " Nowhere are facts relating to the currency so persistently ignored, and fictions so cordially accepted, as in Manchester.   In Liverpool, Birmingham, and Glasgow, a subject which has always been, and is still being, debated by the ablest economists, is still deemed fairly open to discussion.   But in Manchester, and sad to say in this room dedicated especially to such inquiries, a strong banking and bullionist interest has prevented the most important of all questions from being fully discussed."

like other early writers on the trade cycle, Mills broke new ground in several directions; and theorists of different schools can claim affiliation with him. No doubt he over-stressed the periodicity of the cycle, and his division of the so-called normal cycle into three years of decline, three of improvement, three of over-excitement, and one of crisis, was an undue simplification. Longer experience and improved statistics have taught us, on the one hand, that panic is not an inevitable feature of the movement, and on the other, that crises may occur in other places than that assigned to them in the scheme.[1] But, when all this has been said, the fact remains that Mills accomplished a work of originality and laid foundations on which others have built structures of greater elaboration. His essay aroused immediate interest. It was introduced as a text-book in the University of Edinburgh by W. B. Hodson, a member of the Society, who was appointed to the Chair of Political Economy and Mercantile Law in 1871. But its most far-reaching effect was through its influence on the work of Stanley Jevons—an influence generously acknowledged even after Jevons had soared far above the credit structure on his Icarian flight (of which Mills disapproved) into the ether of solar physics.[2]

[1] Wesley Mitchell, *op. cit.*, pp. 379–384.

[2] In a paper of March 1871, " On the Post Panic Period, 1866–1870," Mills gave reasons why cheap money had so far failed to stimulate recovery from the slump; and two years later Elijah Helm entered the field with a paper on " The American Financial Crisis of 1873." Helm's account of the means taken to allay the panic by the issue of clearing-house certificates, and of the subsequent agitation for inflation, are of special interest to a generation that has witnessed the events of 1932–34. But it can hardly be claimed that this paper added anything to the theory of the cycle.

II

Apart from what they had to say on the credit cycle, the Manchester bankers whose work has just been reviewed made pointed comments on matters relating to their own business. It was the period of intense struggle between the private houses and the joint-stock banks, the formation of which had been legalised, in the provinces by the Act of 1826, and in London by that of 1833. Two of the questions at issue in the fifties were whether the liability of the joint-stock banks should be limited or unlimited, and whether interest should, or should not, be paid on deposits. Reference to both was made in a Postscript to William Langton's paper of 1857. Urging that "the greater the responsibility, the greater is likely to be the care and forethought," Langton expressed his hostility to the proposal (to which legislative sanction was given in the following year) that the liability of shareholders in joint-stock banks should be limited. In the other dispute, however, his batteries were ranged alongside those of the company bankers. At this time the joint-stock banks of London were drawing business from the private concerns by the payment of interest, a practice which, it was urged, led the joint-stock bankers to seek a return in speculative channels, and so weakened the structure of the banking system as a whole. But in the provinces, private banks, like Heywood's, also paid interest; and Langton defended this on the ground that, by attracting spare balances, which would otherwise never reach the banks, it effected an economy in the active circulation of notes. T. H. Williams, on the other hand, argued that deposits at call should receive no interest, and that "indeed, no deposits should be received, except on the condition of a certain notice of withdrawal."

From what has been said in the previous section it will be clear that neither Langton nor Williams thought of the Bank Act of 1844 as unduly restrictive; both, indeed, wished to see a pound-for-pound reserve against all notes. But a plea for greater elasticity of issue was made in a paper " On the Bullion Reserve of the Bank of England," read by William Hooley in May 1860, which showed a grasp of the effects of the Act common neither in 1860 nor to-day. The writer pointed out that " whenever a crisis occurs it is not mitigated in the least by the large reserve in the issue department." If six million of coin and bullion were held in the Issue Department, the cost of security to the noteholder would be the loss of the profit that might have come from its employment in trade.

" Substantially, this is the price we pay to secure the convertibility of the note in case of a run from internal panic, a very unlikely contingency; whilst the security of the Bank, itself, whose stoppage could alone make such a contingency actual, is allowed to remain uncared for. . . . I firmly believe that the act, *as administered*, has been beneficial; but its value has consisted in that it has secured to us a larger reserve of bullion at the commencement of each drain than we should otherwise have thought it requisite to hold, and so rendered harmless the suspension of its own provisions when the drain became a panic."

Could the essence of the matter have been better expressed ?

During the seventies several important papers were contributed by officials connected with Manchester banks. Robert Montgomery, of the Manchester and Salford Bank, urged " the futility of taking elaborate precautions about £5 and £10 notes if we do not at the same time protect those who deposit millions and who may be responsible for hundreds of millions more." In his view the banking reserve should never be allowed to fall below £12 millions.[1] But Thomas Moxon, of the Manchester and County Bank, attacked the proposal that the reserve against deposits should be legally

[1] " On the Movements of the Bank of England Reserve in the Last Ten Years," December 1874.

fixed, and pointed out that, under such an arrangement, the reserves would be unavailable when they were needed, so that "the legal reserve line becomes the panic line." [1] The main object of Moxon's paper, however, was to demonstrate that, since 1844, the power of control of the money market by the Bank had weakened, and that the growing divergence between market rate and Bank Rate rendered more difficult the control of the foreign exchanges. His remedy was for the commercial banks to form a pool of £10 millions or £15 millions, to be employed in the discount of bills at not under Bank Rate.

"In times . . . when money appears in excess of bills, as the bills, in which this fund would be invested, come due, the proceeds would be withdrawn from competition. The effect would be the same as when the Bank of England borrows on consols, only all the banks acting together would more rapidly denude the market of its surplus, assimilate the open-market rate to the bank rate of discount, and therefore more promptly turn the exchanges in our favour."

Of greater interest to the student of the evolution of the English banking system were two papers read by Henry Baker of the Manchester and Salford Bank. The first [2] drew attention to the "decrease of principal banks, a distinct movement of consolidation; and increase of branch banks, a distinct and elastic movement of organised diffusion." Tracing the number of bank offices to population in each county, the writer found the agricultural areas more plentifully provided than the manufacturing areas. The relative scarcity of banks in the latter was explained partly by lack of thrift, and partly by the special channels of investment which the manufacturing communities had themselves created. But the question was asked "whether the distance between banks and population, now prevailing over the northern division

[1] "On the Recent Variation between the Bank and the Market Rates of Discount," January 1878.

[2] "On Commercial Bank Diffusion in Provincial England," April 1873.

of England, and particularly over the Lancashire section is not too wide ? "

In his second contribution [1] Baker brought up to date the figures in William Langton's paper of 1857, and subjected to scrutiny Langton's claim that his " commercial balance of account was a measure of the dependence of trade on the Bank." The Other Securities, it was pointed out, consisted, to the extent of more than half, of investments of a more or less permanent character, " the probable outcome of a purely initiatory action," and the Other Deposits also contained " an admixture of uncommercial balances." To Langton's diagram Baker added a new curve representing the amount of " bills discounted " and " temporary advances," separated from the weekly total of Other Securities. This independent Index of the volume of commercial recourse to the Bank showed general correlation with Langton's. In the early seventies, however, a change appeared in the quarterly movement, due to the earlier collection of taxes; and two half-yearly movements asserted themselves, " the first of pressure, and the second of relaxation, corresponding to the new periodic conditions of the greater and lesser accumulations in the Government Treasury." Between 1844 and 1865 the Bank of England had generally had to sustain pressure from trade (*i.e.* Other Securities had usually exceeded Other Deposits); but thereafter the position had been reversed. " Since the breakdown of credit in 1866, the Bank, so to speak, employs in her Trade dealings only what she holds from Trade; while, throughout the twenty-two years preceding, she had employed considerably more." The explanation was to be found in the evolution of the Bank of England into a Central Bank of the modern type.

By 1874 the London bankers' balances totalled 76 per cent. of the reserve and nearly half of the Other Deposits ;

[1] " Observations on a Continuation Table and Chart, showing the Balance of Account between the Mercantile Public and the Bank of England," May 1876.

and if it had been possible to include the balances of the provincial bankers at the Bank of England, the proportions would have been much higher. Thus " the ' other deposits ' of the Bank of England, year by year, have been well-nigh drained of their old general commercial element, and maintained and increased in bulk by the substitution of an essentially different one of bankers' reserves." And this change made it a matter of prudence for the Bank to hold more of her resources either in the reserve or in Government securities, and less in discounts and advances.

In the same year, 1876, the Society reprinted William Langton's paper, along with the well-known essay " On the Frequent Autumnal Pressure in the Money Market," which Jevons had read before the London Statistical Society in 1866. This subject of seasonal fluctuation of discount rate was further discussed in the following session by Sir (then Mr.) R. H. Inglis Palgrave.[1]   In order to issue notes to meet the payment of rents and wages in May and November, the Scottish banks, it was pointed out, were obliged to withdraw gold from the Bank of England at these times. In England a similar demand for more notes arose between August and October; but this was met to a large extent by the issues of the provincial bankers. Himself a note-issuing banker, Palgrave disliked the process by which, under the Act of 1844, the provinces were gradually losing their local issues; and argued that the effect must be a further pressure on the money market.

" The expansions and contractions of the provincial circulation are periodic, and are dependent on the local wants of the population. To connect all these local requirements with the central reserve of the country would introduce increased demands on it, which could only be met by increased fluctuations in the rate of discount."

Palgrave's paper brought a letter [2] from Langton, claiming that his own index of the " commercial balance "

[1] " On the Influence of a Note Circulation in the Conduct of Banking Business."   [2] *Transactions*, 1876–7.

was superior to that of discount rates as " a barometrical guide for the finance of Banking," and defending Peel's legislation of 1844 and 1845.

" It is exceedingly natural," said Langton, " that those banks which still retain the privilege of issuing their own notes should desire to retain it, since it naturally adds to their profits; but it has always been recognised in the great industrial district of Lancashire that it is no essential condition to the wielding of manufacturing and commercial enterprise, and that the banks not possessing this privilege have not stinted their customers of any legitimate accommodation. . . . The note payable on demand and the deposit receipt are equally evidences of debt and equally unsecured; therefore equally liable to be reclaimed if the confidence of the public be shaken, or for other cause. But there can be no doubt that in times of commercial panic there is a greater tendency to run for gold by the note-holder than by the simple depositor, whose receipt is not transferable from hand to hand like the note payable to bearer."

To the argument that if provincial bank notes were supplanted by Bank of England notes, manufacturers and traders would feel every disturbance in the money market, and that rates of interest would be higher, Langton replied by reference to conditions during the period before the resumption of cash payments in 1821.

" My personal memory of trade only extends back to the year 1820; but at that time the Liverpool merchants received nothing but bills in payment from Manchester of their cotton invoices; every such payment, if in what was called promiscuous paper, requiring a calculation of interest to make a settlement per appoint. This practice gradually disappeared with the resumption of cash payments by the Bank of England and the lowering of the standard rate of interest; but if economy of interest of money is to be taken as the special recommendation of any particular kind of circulating medium, this one surely ought to bear the palm! "[1]

At this time William Langton was living in retirement in Essex. But his interest in the Society was as

[1] For an alternative interpretation of this decreased use of bills of exchange as currency in the Manchester area, see A. Redford: *Manchester Merchants and Foreign Trade, 1794–1858* (1934).

lively as ever.   In 1877 he read a paper [1] calling attention to the deficiency of over £3 millions in the assets held against deposits in the Trustee Savings Banks, a large part of which, he said, was due to the allowance of too high a rate of interest to depositors.   Four years later, when the finances of the Savings Banks had been reformed, he returned to the subject in a paper " On Recent Savings Bank Legislation." [2]

This was the last contribution to the *Transactions* made by any of the founders.   For nearly half a century Langton had helped to guide the destinies of the Society ; but he was now in his seventy-ninth year.   Six months later he died.

[1] " Savings Banks," November 1877.   [2] May 1881.

CHAPTER VII

THE WORK OF STANLEY JEVONS AND OTHERS

I

THE session 1865–6 was notable in the Society's annals for the election to membership of William Stanley Jevons. The Professor of History at Owens College, Richard Copley Christie, had recently accepted the Faulkner Chair of Political Economy and Commercial Science; and the addition to his duties made necessary the appointment, in 1863, of an assistant in his department. Through the good offices of his cousin, Henry Roscoe, Jevons was appointed to this post, which carried the obligation of giving tuition to backward students.[1] He was then twenty-eight years of age. He had already begun his investigations into periodic commercial fluctuations; his strangely neglected paper on "The Mathematical Theory of Political Economy" had been presented at the Cambridge meeting of the British Association in the previous year; and he was on the point of publishing his tract on *A Serious Fall in the Value of Gold*, which appeared in April 1863. This work showed such promise that it is small wonder that promotion was rapid. Three years after he came to Manchester Jevons was appointed to the Chair of Logic and Mental and Moral Philosophy; and in 1867 he held the title of Professor and Cobden Lecturer in Political Economy.[2] Joining the Statistical Society in

[1] G. W. Daniels, "Economic and Commercial Studies in the Owens College and the University," *The Manchester School*, Vol. I, No. 1, pp. 5–6.
[2] The title is printed on his paper read before the Society on April 10, 1867.

1865–6, he was elected Vice-President in 1868–9, and from 1869 to 1871 he filled the presidential chair.

The first of his contributions to the *Transactions* was on the control of public utilities.[1] It was in this paper that Jevons laid down the four conditions favourable to state management of industry which have been so frequently quoted, and criticised, by later writers. They are :

" 1. Where numberless widespread operations can only be efficiently connected, united, and co-ordinated in a single, all-extensive government system.

" 2. Where the operations possess an invariable routine-like character.

" 3. Where they are performed under the public eye or for the services of individuals, who will immediately detect and expose any failure or laxity.

" 4. Where there is but little capital expenditure, so that each year's revenue and expense account shall represent, with sufficient accuracy, the real commercial conditions of the department."

Using these canons as his guide to policy, Jevons advocated the purchase by the Government of the Tele-graph Service, and the institution of a Parcel Post—measures the first of which was to be put into effect in the following year, and the second (by a fellow economist, Henry Fawcett) in 1883.

In his next paper Jevons described to the members of the Society the events that had led to the formation of the Latin Union, and the proposals of the French Government for a world-wide uniform currency on the basis of a 25-franc piece.[2]

" In the great scheme of international money," he says, " I consider we are far behind our proper place. It is England that should have suggested free trade in money to the world; it is Manchester that should have suggested it to England, as it has suggested other great ideas before. The unification of currencies

[1] " On the Analogy between the Post Office, Telegraphs, and other Systems of Conveyance of the United Kingdom, as regards Government Control," April 1867.

[2] " On the International Monetary Convention, and the Introduction of an International Currency into this Kingdom," May 1868.

is the appropriate sequel to the introduction of free trade. It is a new step in the *rapprochement* of nations and the spread of civilisation."

Incidentally Jevons gave some of the results of his census into the age of gold coins (his sample covered over 165,000 pieces) and of his weighings of sovereigns on the chemical balance in Roscoe's laboratory at Owens College. The substance of the paper was included in the far more elaborate essay read before the Statistical Society of London later in the year.[1]

Of wider scope was the inaugural address of the session 1869–70,[2] which touched on several of the more controversial problems of the time. Combating the view that existing depression was due to free trade, Jevons reminded his audience that severe unemployment had existed in the years 1841–3, at a time when the tariff was published in the form of a book, and " the arrangements of Providence for the supply of food were improved by an ingenious sliding scale." To those who urged the need of reciprocity treaties he retorted, in words that might well be remembered to-day, " Every act of commerce is a treaty of reciprocity." On the education question, as already mentioned, he declared in favour of compulsion ; on temperance he pronounced against prohibition ; and on the subject of medical charities he expressed the fear that " we may make the Union Hospital so easy of access, and so attractive, that it may lead half way to the Poor House itself."

" The British Poor Law of 1832," he added, " is one of the wisest measures ever concerted by any Government, and we of this generation hardly appreciate what it has saved us from. But I much fear lest any mistaken feelings of humanity should lead

---

[1] " On the Condition of the Gold Coinage of the United Kingdom, with Reference to the Question of International Currency," read November, 1868 ; reprinted in *Investigations in Currency and Finance*, pp. 244–296.

[2] " On the Work of the Society in Connection with the Questions of the Day," November 1869.

us to relax the rigour of its application, and to allow it in one way or other to be circumvented and counteracted."

Of greater scientific interest than any of these early papers was that on " The Progress of the Mathematical Theory of Political Economy, with an Explanation of the Principles of the Theory," contributed in November 1874. Its occasion was the publication of Léon Walras's celebrated work,[1] and in it Jevons reminded his fellow members that, as long ago as 1862, he had himself laid down the fundamental proposition that value depends on utility, and had developed his ideas in the *Theory of Political Economy*, published in 1871. Insisting that " the utility of a commodity is no intrinsic or unchangeable quality, but rather . . . depends upon the quantity of the commodity which has already been consumed," he brings out the distinction between total and final utility, on which the whole of modern economic analysis rests. He lays down what is now known as the law of equi-marginal utilities by saying that " the commodity ought to be so divided and consumed that the final degree of its utility in each employment is the same." And he expresses the theory of value in the words : " The values of things are inversely as the quantities of them given, and therefore directly proportional to the final degrees of utility."

During the later years of his life Jevons was increasingly absorbed in the study of social questions, among which the problem of drunkenness was by no means the least serious. That most powerful of agencies in the struggle against intemperance, the United Kingdom Alliance, had been formed in Manchester in 1853, and had committed itself to the principle of " the Permissive Bill "—Local Option. In the Statistical Society its programme was supported by the Rev. S. A. Steinthal and William Hoyle. Jevons was opposed to it. His paper [2] of March 1876 sought to show the improbability

[1] *Eléments d'Economie Politique Pure.*
[2] " On the United Kingdom Alliance and its Prospects of Success."

that the Permissive Bill would pass the House, and urged that, if it did, attempts to put it into operation would be wrecked by the unwillingness of the ratepayers to provide compensation to publicans.

" A rate of not more than a penny has proved in most places a sufficient bar to that most inoffensive law—the Public Libraries Act. In the parish of Withington, where I reside, a bare majority of the ratepayers could never be got to vote for so necessary an expense as the lighting of the streets. This has been lately done under the authority of the Local Government Board, but I regret to say that the ratepayers still decline to incur the expense of mending the roads."

To the policy of the Alliance in advising its members to vote for no candidate who did not support the Bill, Jevons objected that

" Compromise is of the very essence of legislative change, and as society becomes more diverse and complicated, compromise becomes more and more indispensable. It is the only *modus vivendi* as tastes and opinions gradually diverge. It need hardly be said that reforms of all kinds must be immensely retarded if the supporters of each measure insist upon getting their own scheme first through the House of Commons. Mr. Bright happily protested against trying to drive half-a-dozen omnibuses abreast through Temple Bar, but this is what it will come to if we have many bodies like the Alliance, each trying to have the road to itself. It is especially unfortunate when the first one is a heavy, impractical machine which can neither go forward nor be got out of the way."

Finally, Jevons expressed his preference for attacking the problem of drunkenness by a Sunday Closing Act, by a refusal of all new licences so long as the number of the houses exceeded one to five hundred people, and by the revocation of the grocers' licences and the Beer-shops Act.

" It is difficult to imagine," he added, " how anyone could ever have looked upon facilities for the distribution of liquors as a mode of diminishing intemperance. Competition in all other trades tends to the healthy development of the trade, and the consequent increase of the quantity sold. But in the case of liquors our object is to decrease, not to increase the sale, and we must therefore take the opposite course, and place obstacles in the way of the trade which will make liquors dearer and more troublesome to get. . . . The true mode of reforming the sale of liquor is to diminish competition, and to weed out the ill-conducted houses, until the value of the remaining licences has been so far raised that the holders will not dare and will not have sufficient inducement to tolerate abuses."

In the year in which this paper was read, Jevons left Manchester for University College, London, and six years later his life came to an end, by accidental drowning, at Hastings. No one who knows anything of his writings would claim that any of the more important advances made by him in Statistics, Economics, or Logic, was given to the world through the Statistical Society. But (as Professor Daniels has reminded us [1]) a large part of the work that has made his name famous was published during his Manchester period. *The Coal Question* (1865), *Elementary Lessons in Logic* (1870), *The Theory of Political Economy* (1871), *The Principles of Science* (1874), and *Money* (1875), were all written here; and we may recall with satisfaction that his outstanding contribution to Statistics—the device of the geometrical mean in index numbers—was made shortly after he came to the town.[2] Jevons rightly sought for his discoveries a more extensive circle than that afforded by our *Transactions*. What the Manchester statisticians can claim is that the best of his mature years were spent in their company; that the impact of minds like those of William Langton and John Mills did much to shape his thought; and that the wide audience reached by his books and his papers to the Statistical Society of London listened to the authentic voice of the Manchester School, to which, almost to a man, they belonged.

[1] *Loc. cit.*, pp. 5–6.
[2] In " A Serious Fall in the Value of Gold," April 1863.

THE WORK OF STANLEY JEVONS AND OTHERS   93

II

The existence of a department of Political Economy at Owens College helped to bring the Society into contact with economists in other parts of the country. It was, no doubt, friendship with Jevons that induced Bonamy Price (Drummond Professor of Political Economy at Oxford) to give his paper " On the Doctrine of Rent," in March 1872. This made a sober criticism of Ricardo, denounced the undue stress laid on fertility as the ultimate factor, and emphasised the part played by transport in raising the rent yielded by inferior soils relative to that yielded by lands of high quality. Perhaps its chief interest, however, lay in its definition of rent as " the consideration given for the loan of a wealth-producing machine," and its protest against John Stuart Mill's ascription of the term monopoly to the possession of land.

" The arbitrariness with which it is applied in the case of land will be seen, if we think of how many natural advantages there are of the same general character with that belonging to land, to which no one ever thinks of attaching the word monopoly. . . . And, further, let it be well observed, the possession of agricultural land is distinctly free from the vices of a genuine monopoly; it neither raises prices, nor deteriorates the goods produced. If private property in land were abolished, the price of a loaf would not be a fraction lower, nor would the wheat grown and the cattle reared be better than those we now obtain. The only difference would be one of ownership; the State, and not private persons, would own and receive the rents. . . . Whether that would be a wise or mischievous policy is fairly open to argument. So is communism. Communists may rationally discuss whether it would not be expedient that Mr. Mill should devote his great talents to the service of the commonwealth, and accept equal remuneration with the citizen who carries bricks for building. But in neither discussion would the idea of monopoly enter. . . . The private owner, who, either through his predecessor or through his own efforts, has developed the wealth-producing powers of the machine paid for or inherited, is no more to be branded with monopoly than the great author who has so cultivated the gifts with which nature endowed his mind as to realise large pecuniary results from the sale of his writings."

Another academic visitor to the Society was Professor Leone Levi of King's College, London, whose paper on the " Progress of Morals in England during the last Twenty-five Years," given in February 1884, obviously owed much to the influence of Adolphe Quetelet.   After posing the question " Can we statisticians, who are constantly working in illustrating by reference to positive facts the economic and social condition of the people, likewise photograph in a manner their morals ? ", Levi presented a series of statistical snapshots, or better, of cinematographic pictures, illustrative of the moral condition of the nation.   Statistics of divorces and separations, and those of illegitimacy, were taken as negative evidence of the sense of the " duties of the affections " ; and in both these respects England and Wales were found to compare very favourably with other countries of Europe.   Over a period of twenty years " offences against purity " had diminished so as to show " an absolute moral gain of 26 per cent."   On the other hand, " whilst some improvement is noticeable in the offences against the person, the number of suicides—an evidence of moral cowardice in facing the difficulties of life, and of dereliction of duty—shows a considerable increase."   Offences against duties respecting property had fallen by 8 per cent. during the same period.   But these were shown to vary with the state of trade ; and the connection between economic and moral progress was illustrated by a table showing the number of offences against person and property per shilling of the imports and exports per head.   How far the people of England and Wales failed in the " duties of wisdom and prudence " was indicated by the growing number of offences against the Education Act, and by an increase of no less than 68 per cent. in cases of drunkenness.   And offences against order " would seem to indicate an increasing amount of lawlessness."

" Thus," concludes the writer, " any substantial improvement in certain directions seems marred by a corresponding declension in other directions. One important fact, however, is noticeable, viz. that whilst in those acts which have always been held as offences against moral duties, such as offences against the person and property, there has been a decided decrease, in those acts which have only recently been fully recognised as offences against moral duties, such as drunkenness or non-sending children to school, there has been an increase. It is not that the morals of the people are on the whole worse than they were, but rather that the standard of morals is higher, or that public opinion is less tolerant and more exacting."

The successor of Jevons at Owens was Robert Adamson, who had studied at Edinburgh and Heidelberg, and was twenty-four years of age when appointed to the Chair of Logic, Philosophy, and Political Economy in May 1876. His only contribution to the Society was that of December 1884, on " Some Considerations on the Theory of Money," which is largely concerned with questions of definition. Criticising Mill's statement of the Quantity Theory, Adamson says,

" When . . . an economist tells us that the value of money depends on demand and supply, and that ' the supply of money is all the money *in circulation* at the time,' we must think that he is speaking in enigmas. The value of money is the price of commodities, and it cannot be meant that prices depend on the quantity of its money that a nation employs in the form of legal tender. But if this is not the meaning, the only other interpretation reduces the proposition to the veriest verbal truism, that as money-price is the numerical statement of the quantum of money given for a commodity, money-price is higher or lower according as that quantum is greater or smaller. . . . Certainly the prices of the various classes of other commodities will in one way depend upon the quantity of the common medium which is exchanged for them; they *are* these quantities. . . . The comparative efficiency of a country as one member of the great trading community is what in the long run determines the scale of prices in it, and it is to variations in the conditions affecting its efficiency that we must turn for final explanation of the movements which on the surface appear as changes in an independent entity, Money."

At least as early as 1871 Alfred Marshall had found

the solution to the problem [1] posed in the first part of this quotation; but his extreme reluctance to publish made it possible, till well into our own generation, for acute minds to ask questions similar to those raised by Adamson and to be given no answer.

Adamson's chief interests, it must be confessed, were metaphysical rather than economic. After six sessions' work he was relieved of his lectures in Political Economy; in 1893 he left Manchester to become Professor of Logic at St. Andrews; and two years later he was appointed to the Chair of Logic and Rhetoric in the University of Glasgow.

By this time Owens College had become part of the Victoria University. In 1882, an Irishman, J. E. Crawford Munro, had been elected to the Chair of Law, and on the retirement of Adamson, Munro became Cobden Lecturer in Political Economy. These positions he held until the early nineties, when he left to practise as a barrister in London, though his connection with the town was renewed when, in 1892, and again, in 1895, he stood, unsuccessfully, as Liberal candidate for East Manchester. He died in 1896.

Though Munro had a wide field of knowledge as his province, he is remembered to-day chiefly for his cultivation of a small plot: his dominating interest was in arrangements for making wages vary with the price of the product, or with some other index of the profits of industry. In 1885 he prepared for the British Association a report on " Sliding Scales in the Coal Industry "; and in 1890 he drew up a table of variations of wages under the system for the Royal Commission on Mining Royalties. To the Statistical Society he contributed two papers on the subject. The first of these [2] describes the scales then in operation in the iron industries of Britain and the United States, and urges the extension of the device to mining royalties and agricultural rents.

---

[1] *Memorials of Alfred Marshall* (edited by A. C. Pigou), pp. 28–30.
[2] " Sliding Scales in the Iron Industry," December 1885.

" It seems to me," added Munro, " that the principle of the sliding scale is the greatest discovery in the distribution of wealth since Ricardo's enunciation of the law of rent. . . . Hitherto it has been applied to wages and profits only, but there is no reason why rent of every kind might not be brought within its influence. . . . A rent fixed so as to vary with the price of produce provides for the future as well as the present, and whilst it makes the landlord share in the loss resulting from low prices, on the other hand it gives him a share in the benefit resulting from high prices: it makes the interests of landlords and tenant really identical. It is in the strictest accordance with economic teaching, and it requires no act of the legislature to introduce it as a working principle."

By the year 1889, when his second paper [1] on the subject was read, sliding scales had fallen into disfavour in the coal industry; and Munro was at pains to show that this was due to defects in the particular scales and not to the principle itself. Among the reasons given were the lag between a movement of price and that of wages; the practice of lessees in entering into long contracts for the sale of coal, which prevented wages in many collieries from rising when prices in the open market were advancing; the belief of the miners that a sliding scale tempted employers to under-sell each other, and so kept prices and wages low; and the opposition of trade unionists, on the ground that the system limited their freedom of action. He did not mention among the objections to this second greatest of discoveries in distribution that one expressed by a working collier in the words, " the —— thing has no bottom ! " [2]

Munro's Presidential Address for the session 1890–1 dealt with " The Local Taxation of Chief Rents." For its distinction between the incidence of taxes on ground rents and that of taxes on chief rents, and for its discussion of the principles of " Betterment," it is well worth reading; but it is hardly susceptible of summary.

[1] " Sliding Scales in the Coal and Iron Industries from 1885 to 1889."
[2] Quoted in H. S. Jevons, *The British Coal Trade*, p. 496.

H

It was followed in December 1891 by a paper on " Wages and Hours of Working in the Coal Industry in France, Germany, and England," in which Munro's listeners were warned against assuming that the shorter hours and higher wages of English colliers were injurious to the export trade; that low wages and long hours gave France and Germany an advantage over us; or that the position of the miner would necessarily be improved by either State control or State ownership of minerals.

Some months earlier Munro had resigned the Cobden Lectureship, and for a few years there was no proper provision for the teaching of economic science in Manchester. When the gap was filled it was upon a young man destined to play an important part in British and international statistics that the choice fell. Alfred William Flux, who was to introduce Jevons' geometrical average into the official index number of wholesale prices, was appointed Cobden Lecturer in 1894, and four years later became the first Stanley Jevons Professor of Political Economy in the University.

CHAPTER VIII

SOCIAL CURRENTS, 1870–1900

In recent years the period of mid- and late-Victorian England has been the subject of many brilliant satires. Industry and thrift are not virtues that kindle to enthusiasm to-day; and it is easy to portray sobriety as prudery, and social purpose as organised hypocrisy. Those who delight in exposing the pomposities of the past—as though insincerity and show were things outgrown to-day—might, it must be confessed, find in the *Transactions* features inviting caricature. They might illustrate Victorian pharisaism from a passage [1] describing the galleries of the Paris Exhibition, where, alone among peoples, the English shrouded their exhibits in linen on Sundays, lest French working men should profane the Lord's Day by looking on them. They might quote Leone Levi's " I have no faith that the stage will ever become a public instructor in morals, for the plots rest on, or involve, revenge and murder, seduction and adultery, and the general tone is frivolous in the extreme," either as an example of Victorian Puritanism, or as evidence of the artistic depths to which the English drama had sunk. But, if they were fair, they would mention also the long list of towns where public libraries and museums were open on Sundays; and they would quote the concluding wisdom of William E. A. Axon's paper on expenditure on theatres : [2] " Amusement for the bulk of mankind is not a luxury but a necessity.

---

[1] William E. A. Axon, " Statistical Notes on the Sunday Opening of Libraries and Museums," June 1879.

[2] " The Cost of Theatrical Amusements," June 1882.

Whatever the pecuniary cost of amusement may be it is infinitely cheaper than no amusement at all."

Manchester was compact of the virtues and failings of the age. Those who could see only the latter held the city in hatred and contempt.

> " Taken as a whole," wrote Ruskin,[1] " I perceive that Manchester can produce no good art, and no good literature; it is falling off even in the quality of its cotton; it has reversed and villified in loud lies, every essential principle of Political Economy; it is cowardly in war, predatory in peace; and as a corporate body, plotting at last to steal, and sell, for a profit, the waters of Thirlmere and clouds of Helvellyn."

A community that adorned the walls of its civic centre with the frescoes of Maddox Brown, and that had given warm hospitality for many years to Charles Hallé, could have put up a case against the charge of Philistinism. But perhaps Manchester did not consider it worth while. Thirlmere, on the other hand, was vital to future existence, and members of the Statistical Society were passionate in their support of the scheme. " Manchester," remarked T. R. Wilkinson, " would have to undergo much abuse from crotchet-mongers in every part of the land, because the Corporation have had the wisdom to look ahead to a time when this great industrial centre will require more water than Woodhead can supply." He added that " if it became a question of all England against Manchester, he would be prepared to do his part to support the city authorities." [2]

Similar enthusiasm was shown for another great enterprise which was ultimately to involve the civic powers. " Regarded . . . as a commercial speculation, there can be no doubt whatever of the sound and stable prospects of the Ship Canal," wrote the engineer, Francis Condor,[3] in 1882. " Within a few years of its opening, it is difficult to avoid the conclusion that it will pay

[1] *Fors Clavigera*, LXXXII, p. 298.

[2] Discussion on the Inaugural Address of Thomas Dickens, 1877–78.

[3] " The Actual and Possible Cost of Conveyance between Manchester and Liverpool," November 1882.

$13\frac{1}{2}$ per cent. on the capital." It was in 1882 that, under pressure of bad trade, a member of the Society, Daniel Adamson, took steps to give practical form to the project. The canal was opened to traffic on New Year's Day, 1894, and three years later Woodroofe Fletcher [1] summarised for the Society some of the beneficial results of its operation. If it was already clear that the hope of large dividends must be modified, it was something that over a million tons of merchandise were passing along the canal in a year, and that the railways and other carriers had been forced to make substantial reductions in their freights to and from Manchester. The writer was probably not wrong in attributing to the canal part at least of the revival of local trade that marked the middle nineties.

But it was the wider movements of national life that occupied the greater number of the meetings of the Society. The period saw further advances in political democracy. Foreign competition was beginning to count as a hostile force in British overseas trade. It was the age of Bismarck and of a new concern for national security. Socialism and Imperialism were coming to the fore. Depressed social classes were becoming vocal. And the growth of combinations of both labour and capital was giving rise to a new range of problems. All these changes were mirrored in the *Transactions*, and there were few political or economic events on which members of the Society did not register in print their opinions and comments.

Only a few examples can be given. When, in the forties and early fifties, the question of University reform had first been raised, James Heywood had read to the Society a number of papers on the subject.[2] And

---

[1] " The Economic Results of the Ship Canal on Manchester and the Surrounding District," February 1897.

[2] " Report on the State of Education in Trinity College, Cambridge," 1840–1 ; " On University Education," 1852–3 ; " On the Advantages of the University at Oxford," 1854–5 ; " On Cambridge Academical Statistics," 1855–6.

when, in 1870, Gladstone proposed to remove the religious tests, Professor A. S. Wilkins discussed the problem, and pointed the way to a redistribution of University endowments.[1] The passing of the Trade Union Act and the Criminal Law Amendment Act of 1871 was preceded by a not wholly unsympathetic account of the functions of labour unions by Elijah Helm, who, at this time, assisted Jevons with the evening classes at Owens College;[2] and, during the agitation that followed, G. H. Pownall contributed a paper on the same topic.[3]

Another great working-class movement also aroused discussion. The setting up in Manchester of the Co-operative Wholesale Society, in 1864, had been followed by a big extension of retail societies on the Rochdale pattern, and the movement was beginning to attract the attention of many who could hardly be described as working men. In 1872 the shopkeepers of London became so alarmed that they petitioned the Chancellor of the Exchequer to suppress the Civil Service Stores, and threatened to give up trading with every wholesaler who supplied it with goods. In the Statistical Society the leading exponent of co-operative principles was Dr. John Watts, who had been a member of Robert Owen's Queenwood community, and had edited, for a time, a periodical with the provocative title of *The Blasphemer*. For many years, however, Watts had given his best energies to the cause of elementary and University education in Manchester, and was now a zealous member of the new School Board. It was no communistic reorganisation of humanity that he advocated in his paper[4] of 1872 : his hope was merely for some exten-

[1] " On University Endowments and the Higher Education of the Nation," November 1870.

[2] " On Trades Unions in Relation to National Industry," February 1871.

[3] " Some Considerations Affecting the Relations of Capital and Labour," March 1879.

[4] " On Co-operation Considered as an Economic Element in Society," November 1872.

sion of self-governing workshops and of profit-sharing with employees.

"Whether pure co-operation extends into productive employments, or causes the system of sharing profits with workmen to be generally adopted by employers, it will probably lead to the abolition of strikes and lockouts on the subject of wages; will promote economy of waste, and improve the quality of workmanship on piece-work; and, by establishing a conviction in the minds of day workers that it is to their interest to do as much instead of as little as possible during working hours, will prove highly beneficial to society."

A few years later Vansittart Neale, the Christian Socialist lawyer, reinforced the argument and dealt with the subject of co-operation in its wider aspects.[1]

The publication of Henry George's *Progress and Poverty* led to a revival, in the eighties, of interest in questions of the Land. Papers on the subject were read by the Rev. W. A. O'Connor, and by Dr. Pankhurst in 1883.[2] A few years later the privileges of landlords were discussed by R. C. Richards and T. H. Elliott;[3] and, in the early nineties, the Rev. Harold Rylett put the case for the Taxation of Land Values, and W. H. S. Watts (President 1894–5) contributed a valuable paper on "Betterment, Worsement, and Recoupment."

A work of greater moment than that of Henry George was Charles Booth's *Labour and Life of the People* (1889), which led a member of the Society, Fred Scott, to make a detailed inquiry into poverty in two working-class districts of Manchester and Salford.[4] The "very poor" were defined as those with an income of less

---

[1] "The Social Aspects of Co-operation," March 1887.

[2] "Our Land Laws," March 1883; "The Land and the Nation," December 1883.

[3] "A Consideration of Some of the Effects of the Landlord's Preferential Position upon Commerce and Agriculture," January 1888; "Notes on Taxation and Rating," February 1888.

[4] "The Condition and Occupations of the People of Manchester and Salford," May 1889.

than 4s. *per adult* per week; the "poor" as those with
not more than 6s. 3d.; and the "comfortable" as those
with 8s.

"Those whose occupations are stated number 4,440. Of
these, 1,663, or 37·4 per cent., are very poor—that is to say,
they have not the means of independent subsistence, 582, or 13·1
per cent., are poor—that is, they have the means of procuring bare
necessaries only, and cannot, from their means, indulge in any
recreation involving cost, or in any of the comforts enjoyed by
those better off; 663, or 14·9 per cent., are returned as comfortable,
while 1,532, or 34·5 per cent., are not classified."

And this was in a period of good trade and full employment.

Political events, in the narrower sense, gave rise to
many papers. The introduction of the third Reform
Bill was the occasion of a protest against the breaking
up of counties and towns into single-member con-
stituencies, and of a plea for Proportional Representation made by Lonsdale Broderick.[1] Childers' ill-con-
sidered scheme to convert the 3 per cent. stock might
perhaps have been more successful if the Chancellor of
the Exchequer had paid attention to the observations of
Henry Baker[2] made in January 1884. Perhaps, however, the most momentous topic of discussion of these
years was that arising out of the attacks on the established fiscal policy and the desire for a closer union with
the British colonies. In 1877 Stephen Bourne had
welcomed the growing dependence of Britain upon
foreign supplies of food, on the ground that it brought
a more varied diet, opened up new markets for exports,
and tended towards international friendship.[3] But a
few months later he sounded a note of alarm:

"It will no longer do to act upon the maxim—'Take care of
the imports and let the exports take care of themselves.' This

[1] "Proportional Representation," February 1885.
[2] "On the Revaluation by the State of the Three Per Cent. Annuity
on the National Debt."
[3] "On the Increasing Dependence of this Country upon Foreign
Supplies of Food," April 1877.

did well enough when the world was pressing upon us to supply it with its wants—not now, when we have to press our wares upon the world. The coming leader of the state," he added, " will have a problem to solve of far higher moment than the support of dynasties, the maintenance of the balance of power, the rectification of frontiers, however important these may be. He must find out how to feed the people at home, how to people our possessions abroad. The man who shall thus rectify this balance of trade, and of population, will be the greatest benefactor with which England, her colonies, and possessions, the united British Empire, has ever been blessed." [1]

Already Disraeli aspired to become this benefactor. In 1869 the Reciprocity Association had come into being; and a few years later the Imperial Federation League had been formed by W. E. Forster, with the support of men of such varied views as the Earl of Rosebery, Lord Brassey, Sir John Lubbock, James Bryce and Professor J. R. Seeley. In January 1887 a Member of Parliament, Howard Vincent, addressed the Society on the programme of the League.[2]

" Our empire," he remarked, " was obtained mostly by our ships and our guns pointed by true British eyes. There are as yet no signs, with the hand of all continental Europe on the sword hilt, of the speedy advent of that millennium when we shall be able to keep our own by other means than English courage and Sheffield steel."

The path to Federation lay, he declared, in closer trading relations with the colonies. He looked forward

" to a reciprocity of tariffs—to the day when free trade means free trade. To-day it is in too many states—Sell everything to England, but buy nothing English. But as regards Greater Britain we can patiently abide our time . . . federated in peace and in war, we have nothing to fear from the protective tariffs and the arms of all the world combined."

A few days before the meeting the President, Thomas

[1] " On the True Relation in which Imports and Exports should Stand to Each Other in the Trade of a Prosperous Country."
[2] " The British Empire and Imperial Federation," January 1887.

B. Moxon, had sent John Bright an invitation to be present, and this produced the following reply, which was published in nearly every important newspaper in the country.[1]

DEAR SIR,

I have to thank you for your invitation to the " federation " meeting fixed for the 21st of this month. I cannot attend the meeting, and regret to say that I have no sympathy with its object and purpose. I am as anxious as you and your friends can be that the colonies should remain attached to and in perfect friendship with the mother country, but I am of opinion that any attempt to unite them by political bonds more closely than we are now connected will tend not so much to permanent union as to separation. England will not be governed or in any way influenced in her policy by Canada or Australia or the Cape. The colonies will allow of no interference by England with them, with their laws, or their tariffs. England's blind foreign policy may involve us in wars with some or with several of the European Powers—wars in which the colonies have no interest, but by and through which they may be subjected to serious injury. In such case what will happen ? The federation cord will be strained to the uttermost, it will probably break; the colonies will prefer separation and freedom to the burdens and sufferings which their connection with a European nation through their mother country will impose upon them. How would your federation deal with the fisheries dispute between Canada and the United States ? If Canada were an independent State the dispute would soon be settled, for she would yield to the arguments of her powerful neighbour, and if there were no " Dominion " of Canada the dispute would be settled by English concession of the reasonable claims of the Government at Washington. How would a federation composed of delegates or representatives from the colonies of Australia, from South Africa, from Canada, and perhaps from India, meeting and acting with some representative body in England, deal with this fisheries question and with other questions which might and would arise within the wide boundaries of our ever-growing Empire ? I commend a consideration of these problems to any thoughtful men—men who are active in promoting a federation league. The federation project seems to me to be founded on ignorance alike of history and geography. It is partly or mainly the offspring of the Jingo spirit which clamours for a vast and continually widening Empire, and seems almost ready to boast that it can

[1] *Manchester Guardian*, January 15, 1887.

fight the world outside its own limits.   I would recommend all
sensible men to let the question rest.   If we are conciliatory and
just to the colonies, and if our foreign policy is less mad than it
has been during much of the present century, we may hope that
the friendship between Britain and her daughter States may long
continue and may strengthen.   If dangers come which we cannot
now foresee, but from which nations cannot escape, and if separation
becomes necessary, let us hope that what will be done will be done
in peace and with a general concurrence, and that the lustre of
the English name and fame will not be tarnished, but will receive
an added glory from the greatness and the prosperity and the
wisdom of the States which England has founded.

I am, very respectfully yours,
JOHN BRIGHT.

Probably most of those who listened to Vincent's
paper were willing to take John Bright's advice and let
the matter rest.   But the fact that it should have been
possible to ask such questions in a Society to which
Richard Cobden had belonged can hardly have left the
minds of the older members undisturbed.   It was
portentous of storms ahead.

CHAPTER IX

THE COTTON INDUSTRY AND POPULATION STATISTICS

To leave the impression that, during the late years of Victoria, the Society was concerned only with the changing political scene would be a serious injustice. Much work of a more detached character was done in the last decades of the nineteenth century; and if less space is given to this, it is only because the more purely statistical papers hardly lend themselves to quotation and summary. On two topics in particular, contributions of permanent value were made. A series of papers on the Cotton Industry, and another on the statistics of Population, deserve special treatment.

In 1877 Joseph Spencer set forth the indices of the growth of the cotton industry during the past half-century.[1] Between 1825 and 1875 Britain's consumption of raw cotton had increased eightfold, while that of the Continent had grown ninefold, and that of the United States still more. Whereas in 1830 the proportion of the crop consumed by Britain had been 57·3 per cent., in 1875 it was only 47·0 per cent. Such figures were, however, misleading. The absolute increases in the weight of raw cotton used showed the superior progress of Britain; for consumption had increased here by 1,016 million lb., against an increase of continental consumption of 737 million lb., and of American consumption of 501 million lb. Moreover, the number of spindles in the United Kingdom had grown from 9 to 37·5 millions, while in Europe the increase had been only

[1] " The Growth of the Cotton Trade in Great Britain, America, and the Continent of Europe, during the Half-century ending with the Year 1875," June 1877.

from 2·8 to 19·5 millions, and in the United States from 1·2 to 9·5 millions. And, since the average counts of yarn were higher here than in other countries, the figures under-stated the advantage which Britain held over her competitors. It required, therefore, no great act of faith for the writer to conclude:

" If in spite of hostile, in some cases prohibitory tariffs, with our market open to receive the productions of other countries without hindrance; and with the other markets of the world as open to them as to us, we retain the pre-eminence; we may cherish the hope that by faithfully cultivating and exercising those qualities that have given us this rank, we shall in the future retain the lead, until the supplies of coal and iron, the foundation of our success, are practically exhausted."

If the long view gave rise to optimism, a scrutiny of recent years gave rise to some concern. In 1878 Elijah Helm pointed out [1] that " last season our own consumption of the raw material was rather less than it was seven years ago. Within the same period the consumption of the continent has increased upwards of 26 per cent., and that of the United States nearly 39 per cent." But this was during a period of special depression, and such comments as were made on the Cotton Industry during the next few years were, on the whole, cheerful. John Fielden commended the manufacturers of North-East Lancashire for their intelligence in uniting, in 1882, to tide over a temporary depression by organised short-time working; [2] and another writer spoke with pride of the financing of Oldham mills out of the savings of the operatives. If things went wrong, it was the custom to blame extraneous factors, such as the currency: every depression brought a spate of papers on Bimetallism or the rehabilitation of silver.[3] In 1892, it is true,

[1] *Loc. cit.*

[2] " On the Employment of Surplus Labour, more especially during Periods of Commercial Depression," April 1882.

[3] " In this city the double standard is being held out to the spinners and manufacturers like a piece of juicy meat on a prong before a hungry pack, and you may imagine how Oldham, Burnley, etc. bay and howl."

William Fogg [1] called attention to the serious effects of the growing exports of textile machinery; spoke in words, strange to modern ears, of the intrusion of our Indian competitors into the market of Japan; and declared that any further shortening of hours of labour in Lancashire would lead to higher costs of production and a loss of trade. But this was on the dark eve of the twenty-weeks strike which ended in the Brooklands Agreement. When, in the following session, Frederick Merttens presented one of the most comprehensive papers [2] on the Cotton Industry ever read to the Society, he was loud in his praise of the conduct of the operatives.

" The basis of our wealth, intelligence and culture is broadening; the pauper cotton ' hand ' of the thirties and forties is rapidly becoming the respectable middle-class citizen of to-day. . . . The patience and fortitude, the orderliness of the cotton operatives and coal miners under the recent lockouts were the admiration of the civilised world and deservedly enlisted the sympathy of their fellow-men. . . . The wisdom and moderation shown so far by Trade Unionists encourage the hope that they will not push their demands beyond reason and the best interests of the country. They fully recognise the importance of our foreign trade, and are not likely to injure their own condition by driving it into the hands of our competitors."

The paper is full of figures demonstrating the cheapening of production, the reduction in the number of operatives per thousand spindles, and the increase of looms per weaver. To obtain "the same conveniences for which English operatives lay out their wages at free-trade prices " the German workman would have had to work $15\frac{3}{4}$ to $19\frac{3}{4}$ hours, the French $18\frac{1}{4}$, the Eastern Bohemian $41\frac{1}{4}$ hours, for every 9 hours worked in Lancashire. So far from fearing an eight-hour day the

---

John Mills to W. B. Hodson, September 1875. *From Tinder-box to the " Larger " Light*, p. 330.

    [1] " Workers in Cotton Factories and the Eight Hours Day," November 1892.
    [2] " The Hours and Cost of Labour in the Cotton Industry at Home and Abroad," session 1893-4.

writer insisted that " any reduction in wages or increase in working hours would mean more than a corresponding reduction in production," and concluded that " shorter hours will again increase the energy, the vitality, the productiveness of our workers on which alone depends the victory in the industrial struggle."

Discussion of the statistics of population during this period was almost entirely the work of one man. Thomas Abercrombie Welton joined the Society in 1870 and remained a member till his death in 1918. Though he lived in London and was active in the Royal Statistical Society, he was second only to John Roberton in the number of his contributions to our *Transactions*, and his papers extended from the session 1871–2 to that of 1914–15. The first of these [1] called attention to an estimate Welton had made, in a paper to the British Association, of the probable excess of females that would be revealed when the Census of 1871 was published. This was considerably lower than that suggested by the Registrar-General; and the published returns proved that he had been right. Either the emigrants of 1861–71 had included a higher proportion of females than formerly, or the immigrants must have embraced an unusual number of males. Welton opposed the payment from the public purse of grants for emigration, and urged that " if English people were helped across the Atlantic, something like corresponding numbers of Irish and foreigners would be attracted to take their places." Emigration, he insisted, should be " an opportunity for the adventurous, rather than a resource for the despairing."

In a paper [2] of 1874 William E. A. Axon declared that " one of the most painful adjuncts to European civilisation are those thousands of women who can never become mothers and wives, and to whom so many of the ordinary roads to fortune and fame are barred by social prejudice and caste feeling." The same topic was

---

[1] " On Some Published Results of the Census of 1871," Session 1871–2.

[2] " On the Relative Proportion of the Sexes," March 1874.

pursued by R. Bailey Walker in the following year.[1] The excess of females was put at upward of half a million, and it was pointed out that when widowers re-married they usually chose their partners from those who had had no previous experience of matrimony. " Where one bachelor had married a widow, two widowers had married spinsters."

These papers brought Welton to Manchester post haste. In his " Notes on the Relative Number of the Sexes amongst Emigrants "[2] he showed the danger of looking at the gross figures only, instead of having regard to age and civil condition. " No doubt," he said, " there are many thousands of marriageable persons of either sex who cannot marry, but this is rather consequent upon want of means than the result of any scarcity of persons of the opposite sex." His figures indicated that the surplus did not consist of unmarried women between twenty and forty years of age, but rather of widows and spinsters of forty and upward. In another paper[3] of the same year he showed that the excess of *unmarried* females over unmarried males above the age of fifteen was only 62,000, and concluded that there was no superfluity worth speaking of below the age of thirty-five. Examination in detail showed that such excess as existed was in general distributed geographically according to the demand for female labour. But in Lancashire and Yorkshire it was small, and in colliery areas there was an actual deficiency of single women.

Bailey Walker had drawn inferences from a table showing the proportion of the population that had attained the age of ninety in the various Census districts. He had asserted that where the northern and midland districts had preserved one person to the age of ninety, the Welsh had preserved two, and the south-western and eastern counties were " more than twice as conservative of their aged people, in comparison with the metropolitan

---

[1] " On the Facts of the Census " (Vol. III), February 1875.
[2] March 1875.
[3] " On the Proper Meaning of Certain Statistical Facts," June 1875.

districts." That of Lancashire and Cheshire was far beyond all other districts in "its deadly results." Again, Welton made pertinent comment:

"How can it be expected," he asked, "that in districts from whence the young and active have emigrated, the proportion of aged shall be as low as it is in the districts to which those young persons have gone? The old men of Lancashire are the survivors from a time when the county was much less populous and the births proportionally few. The old men of less progressive districts are the representatives of births, perhaps, within a little as numerous as at present."

If, instead of looking at the numbers of the aged, one considered the mortality rate of persons between sixty-five and eighty-five, Lancashire and Cheshire did not show up so badly.

In two papers [1] of the following session Welton surveyed the main changes in the occupations of the people over the past twenty years, pointing to the decline in the number of agricultural labourers and the phenomenal increase in that of miners and metal workers. Following the repeal of the "taxes on knowledge" there had come about a growth in the number of printers; and other expanding occupations were those of domestic and Government service. "The first conclusion to be derived from the Census seems to be, that the greatest increase of workers has taken place in those departments of industry where machinery can hardly be brought into use, or where it plays a subordinate part" and "the changes in the distribution of our population . . . appear to have been brought about, to a great extent, by a new direction being almost imperceptibly given from time to time to the employment and migrations of young people."

A few years later Welton called attention [2] to the tide of migration from the south-western counties of Wiltshire, Somerset, Devon, and Cornwall, and from the eastern counties of Norfolk and Suffolk. Between 1851 and

[1] "On the English Census of Occupations, 1871," January 1876.
[2] "Stationary Populations," February 1880.

I

1871 the area had been " denuded of nearly one-half of the native male population which would have been found there at the ages twenty-five to forty, supposing no migration whatever had taken place." In these circumstances, he concluded once more, there was no need for governmental assistance to emigration.

Lancashire, on the other hand, was a centre of immigration, and in his Presidential Address of 1881 Henry Baker [1] set at 200,000 the number of persons who had come to the county from outside during the past decade. If Manchester itself showed a slight decrease of numbers, this was due to the error of the Registrar-General in " adhering to town areas, which have been long outgrown by their extending populations." Greater Manchester had increased by 20 per cent.—a growth which Welton [2] declared to be " very satisfactory, when we bear in mind the fluctuating fortunes of all such great aggregations of humanity, and the difficulties in the way of a large *relative* increase of that which is already enormous."

Towards the end of the century the tendency to a falling birth-rate gave rise to much concern. In a paper [3] full of subtle argument, R. H. Hooker demonstrated its relation to a prior fall in the marriage-rate. He attributed it not—as other writers did—to trade depression, or the decline of agriculture, but to a tendency on the part of minors to postpone marriage (one of the most salutary results of the spread of education that followed the act of 1870) and to a decrease of illegitimacy.

In 1898 Welton [4] dealt with a subject that had engaged his attention forty years earlier—the unsatisfactory character of the classification of occupations introduced in the Census of 1851.

" Being at a loss for some plan, the Census Commissioners had recourse to the index of the contents of the Great Exhibition in

[1] " On the Growth of the Manchester Population," November 1881.
[2] " On the Published Results of the Census of 1881," March 1882.
[3] " Is the Birth-Rate Still Falling ? " January 1898.
[4] " On Forty Years Industrial Changes in England and Wales," March 1898.

Hyde Park, and thus arrived at their sub-divisions under the animal, vegetable and mineral substances worked upon, which had the effect of classing greengrocers with cotton manufacturers, and butchers with workers in silk."

The census tables of 1891 showed that substantial improvement in classification had been made; but Welton pressed, in particular, for a separation of those engaged wholly in production from those whose principal function was distribution. His account of the changes in occupations between 1851 and 1891 is a mass of detail that defies summary. Suffice it to say that it makes clear such broad movements as the decline of agriculture, the rise in relative importance of commerce, mining, and metal working, and the marked increase in women's work that resulted from the spread of such technical devices as the typewriter, the sewing machine, and the telephone.

Preoccupation with the problems of population did not, however, exclude other interests. The last decade of the century was fruitful of papers on economic topics which involved the use of statistical method. The returns of the Bankers' Clearing House and the railways, the indices of discount rates, and the prices of commodities and stocks, were made the basis of a " Theory of the Yearly Trade Movement," by Henry Binns.[1] With the help of L. L. Price, Sir William Houldsworth made a survey of Index Numbers,[2] and James Niven discussed the rates of mortality of workers in Lancashire industries.[3] The bicentenary of the Bank of England, and the jubilee of the Bank Charter Act in 1894, led Professor Flux to make his investigation [4] into the accounts of the Bank of England ; and the passing of the Workmen's Compensation Act was the occasion of his paper on " Compensation for Industrial Accidents," read in April 1898. Perhaps the most important of

[1] December 1894.
[2] " Index Numbers and the Course of Prices," March 1897.
[3] " On the Statistics of some Lancashire Industries," April 1899.
[4] " Fifty Years' Accounts of the Bank of England," January 1895.

Flux's contributions, however, was his study of price movements derived from trade returns.[1] By an ingenious method of computation he was able to obtain an index number of the prices of exports extending back to the eighteenth century, which is of permanent value not only to statisticians, but to that growing body of students who are seeking to rewrite economic history on the basis of numerable facts.

[1] " Some Old Trade Records Re-examined : A Study in Price Movements during the Present Century," February 1899.

CHAPTER X

THE TWENTIETH CENTURY

In the early years of the new century one seems to detect a change of note in the voices of those who addressed the Society. In political and economic matters alike the old certitudes were giving way to doubts and hesitations. The fact that it had required an army of a quarter of a million British to subdue a hundred thousand Boers had given a shock to those who believed in the natural superiority of our race. At the Annual Dinner in 1901 Earl Grey stated " that of 11,000 men who had volunteered from the Manchester district for service in South Africa, 8,000 were rejected as unfit to carry a rifle and endure the fatigues and privations of a campaign; and that of the 3,000 who were accepted only 1,200 were pronounced by the Military Authorities to be up to the standard of what a soldier ought to be." Such conclusions revived interest in questions of physical training and hygiene, and were the occasion of a paper by Fred Scott urging the institution of a Ministry of Health.[1] The author was Secretary to the Manchester and Salford Sanitary Association, which had just celebrated its jubilee and had presented a petition to Parliament (through Sir William Houldsworth), asking that physical training should be promoted " on a scale coextensive with the school system of the country."

A few years later, Miss Mary Dendy dealt with the even more vital problem of mental hygiene.[2] In opposi-

[1] " The Case for a Ministry of Health," 1902-3.
[2] " The Problem of the Feeble-minded," March 1908. Miss Dendy had already given a paper on the same subject in 1898. She was not the

tion to those who held that defective children were the product of under-feeding, she asserted that " under-feeding is a result, and not a cause, of weakness of intellect "; and her comment on the general attitude to the feeble-minded deserves to be remembered :

" If a man cannot take care of his family we do not prevent his having a family to take care of, we take care of it for him. . . . And we entirely overlook the fact that the trouble from which he is suffering is hereditary and incurable. . . . If we will play Providence we must be wise as well as pitiful, and we must remember that if the ne'er-do-weels of society have their rights, so have the well-doers."

At the same time changes in industrial structure were the cause of concern. The growth of trusts and combines, of pools and shipping rings, of consolidations of labour and capital, raised problems of business and public policy. Sydney John Chapman, who had succeeded Flux in the Stanley Jevons Chair of Political Economy, called attention to some of them in his eloquent plea for a Faculty of Commerce at the University.[1]

" Business and public functions," he said, " have come to be carried on under the law of the survival of the quickest and most convenient methods. . . . The man who works like a machine, as part of a machine which he does not understand, works badly. And then, as regards the lower clerks, no man is born to be only a clerk. If the upper posts in the business world cannot be recruited from the ranks, then woe betide the ranks and the business world."

---

only woman to address the Society in these years. In a " Talk about the Drama," in December 1910, Miss Horniman answered the question, often asked, as to why she had settled on Manchester for her Repertory Theatre. It was because she liked the people. " Many years ago, she and a couple of friends went on tour with the Irish Plays, and came here to sell books and programmes. . . . The Manchester people did treat one fairly ; when they came and took up her time, they bought a book, and when they wanted to know a great deal, when they talked a really long time, they bought a bound book. It was settled in ten minutes' discussion which of the great cities she should come to."

[1] " On Education for Business and Public Life," February 1902. In the following year he described the complications of local merchanting in his paper on " The Conditions and Consequences of Market Developments in the Cotton Trade," January 1903.

The argument was strengthened by developments in foreign countries. In 1903 Germany had suddenly raised her tariff barrier, and a new menace to Lancashire's trade had appeared. Gustav Jacoby [1] described the events that had brought this about, and urged the need of a specialised body to negotiate commercial treaties with foreign countries. " There is a widespread opinion in commercial circles that had there been a staff of competent experts engaged on the Anglo-French negotiations of 1881 the Cobden Treaty would have been renewed." German and American competition were also the subject of Frederick Mertten's Presidential Address [2] of 1903, and of three important papers by Barnard Ellinger.[3] The first of these made suggestions for the reform of our methods of compiling foreign trade returns. The second pointed out that, in spite of all impediments, Germany was still our second largest customer, as she was also our second largest source of supply ; and that in years of depression our exports to Germany suffered less, and in years of expansion they expanded more, than exports in general. The third showed the remarkable amplitude of the fluctuations of American trade ; it brought out the serious effects of American tariffs, but urged discretion in adjusting our own fiscal policy.

" Before you pass any architect's plan for demolition, alterations, or repairs, be quite sure that you have counted the cost, and that you have fully grasped the value and importance of the old building and the uses to which it is put."

Long before this the tariff question had become a matter of party politics, and members had been guilty of infringing the Constitution of the Society when they

[1] " The German Tariff Maze and Most-Favoured-Nations Systems," February 1903.
[2] " Productivity, Protection, and Integration of Industry," November 1903.
[3] " Value and Comparability of English and German Foreign Trade Statistics," March 1904 ; " An Analysis of our Trade with Germany," November 1908 ; " Our Trade with the United States of America," December 1909.

invited a Member of Parliament, Frederick Platt-Higgins, to give his views on free trade.[1] Far more in accord with the intentions of our founders was the paper in which Hilaire Belloc, at that time also a Member of Parliament, called attention to the virtue of elasticity in tariff systems.[2] Our own tariff, he pointed out, was singularly lacking in this quality; for it had been, for more than a generation, virtually fixed, and at the end of the nineteenth century 90 per cent. of the customs revenue had been obtained from the four staple articles of wine, spirits, tea and tobacco. But trade was changing; new products, like petrol, were becoming commercial necessities. Unless these were taxed, we should find ourselves with a " fossilised system of tariffs not corresponding to the real trade movement of our community."

More serious than that of tariffs was the problem of growing armaments. In December 1911, F. W. Hirst[3] declared that " Mr. Lloyd George's Budget found favour as the ' People's Budget ' not so much because it fleeced the rich as because it gave old-age pensions. But it was really the greatest armour-plate budget of modern times." He pointed out that we were spending the whole produce of our income tax on the Navy, and were heading for a war " which would send Consols below 60, which might end by doubling the national debt, and would probably throw half our people out of employment."

During the pre-war years a variety of industrial and financial problems was brought to the attention of members. A number of attempts to corner the supplies of raw cotton, and the growth of spinning factories in the United States, led the Oldham Chamber of Commerce to take the initiative in setting up the British Cotton

[1] " The Rise and Decline of the Free Trade Movement," December 1905.
[2] " The Elasticity of a Tariff," December 1907.
[3] " The Theory and Finance of Modern Armaments," December 1911.

Growing Association, the activities of which were described by J. A. Hutton [1] in February 1904. Another local institution, the Ship Canal, was the subject of a valuable paper by James S. McConechy.[2] Concern for banking security led Drummond Fraser to urge the holding of more gold and less securities in the issue department of the Bank of England.[3] And A .W. Flux [4] and G. I. Murray [5] dealt with the rise in the yield of gilt-edged securities, and showed the connection between rates of interest and wholesale prices.

But, as ever, the dominant interest of the Society lay in social problems. In November 1901, Max Hesse gave an account of the work of the Jewish Board of Guardians in making small loans to the poor; [6] and in 1904 James Long described the rise of the garden village.[7] In both the economic and the political field the labour movement was advancing. Professor Chapman considered the theoretical limits to which, by concerted action, wages might be raised; [8] and A. H. Gill described how the Taff Vale decision had brought into being a fourth party, which, a few months later, was to occupy twenty-nine seats at Westminster.[9] Ever since 1889, when Lord Dunraven's Committee had reported on the subject, public opinion had been growing less tolerant of the evils of sweating. In 1908 a Select Committee was set up to consider the special problems of the home worker; and in 1910 Chapman [10] demonstrated

[1] "The Work of the British Cotton-Growing Association," February 1904.
[2] "The Economic Value of the Ship Canal to Manchester and District," November 1912.
[3] "The Problem of the Gold Reserve," November 1911.
[4] "The Yield of High-Class Investments, 1896–1910," February 1911.
[5] "The Causes of the Fall in Consols," December 1913.
[6] "On the Effective Use of Charitable Loans to the Poor, without Interest."
[7] "The Garden Village of the Small Holdings Association," April 1904.
[8] "Some Aspects of the Theory of Wages in relation to Practice," January 1905.
[9] "The Organisation of Labour as a Political Force," February 1905.
[10] "Home Work," January 1910.

the weak strategic position of this class of labour, and called attention to the benefits which might flow from the Trade Boards set up in the previous year. In particular, these might act insensibly as councils of improvement, and as representative organs of thought on behalf of the trades concerned—functions that Chapman was to help to extend by the part he played, during the war, in setting up Joint Industrial Councils under the Whitley scheme.

In 1910 Sidney Webb [1] visited the Society to press the claim for the reform of the Poor Law in accordance with the recommendations of the Minority of the Commissioners who had reported in the previous year. He called attention to the rise, since 1834, of new authorities (some of which have been mentioned in earlier chapters) to deal with the education, health, and comfort of the poor. And he spoke of " the far greater fulfilment of parental obligation in the Manchester slum of to-day " (not in spite of, but because of, the intervention of the public powers) " as compared with that which a microscopic observer might have detected in the ' Little Ireland ' of our grandfathers."

The problem of the casual labourer was discussed by R. Williams [2] in a paper concerned with an important experiment in decasualisation he had recently conducted at the Liverpool Docks; and, in the same session, J. L. Paton [3] dealt with the allied problem of the youth " too big for toffy but not quite big enough for baccy, and mighty independent with his 6s. a week—too old to be controlled by the home authorities, but not yet grown up enough to have fallen under the gentler sway of the girl he walks out with on Sundays." In the same year C. F. Bickerdike summarised the results of the recent Board of Trade inquiries into wages and the cost of living

---

[1] " The Economics of the Existing (or of any) Poor Law," October 1910.

[2] " The Organisation of the Casual Labour Market," January 1912.

[3] " The Adolescence of the Working Lad in Industrial Towns," March 1912.

in the United Kingdom and certain foreign countries;
and in March 1914, Professor Chapman and A. N.
Shimmin [1] dealt with the movements of labour between
industries. Their paper, which is of interest to statisticians as much for its methods as for its results, showed
that inflows and outflows from particular occupations
took place on a considerable scale, and were associated
with the needs of particular industries for workers of
particular ages. In these circumstances the cul-de-sac
occupation was an economic necessity. But, since it
involved a costly sacrifice of many young people,

" the establishment of labour-training institutes becomes doubly
necessary, and an added importance attaches to Labour Exchanges
with special reference to the claims of the rejected of certain
trades whom it is essential to deal with before they become demoral-
ised or suffer in vigour or spirit."

The remainder of the *Transactions* must be treated in
the barest summary, for it is no part of the work of the
historian to appraise the achievements of his contem-
poraries. Between 1914 and 1919 the activities of the
Society were necessarily curtailed. But in February
1915, the aged Thomas Welton made an analysis (which
filled 130 pages of the *Transactions*) of the " Occupations
of the People of England and Wales in 1911, from the
Point of View of Industrial Developments "; Monsignor
Poock [2] dealt with the falling birth-rate and with infant
mortality; and Eric B. Nathan [3] presented a new Life
Table showing the mortality in Lancashire during 1911
and 1912. Problems of the future were discussed by
Barnard Ellinger,[4] who put the case for a Guild of
Shippers; by Mrs. Annot Robinson,[5] who dealt with the

[1] " Industrial Recruiting and the Displacement of Labour," March
1914.
[2] " Certain Influences Affecting the National Rate of Population,"
November 1917.
[3] " Lancashire Vital Statistics as Disclosed by the 1911 Census,"
January 1918.
[4] " The Case for a Guild of Shippers, with some Suggestions," March
1917.
[5] " The Substituted Labour of Women, 1914–1917," December 1917.

substitution of women for men in industry; and by Bishop
Casartelli,[1] who stressed the importance of the study of
foreign languages, and protested against the narrow-
mindedness revealed in the fall in the number of students
of German.   Sir Norman Hill [2] described the past of
British Shipping; and David Halliwell [3] considered the
future of British Railways.   But for scholarship the most
important papers of these years were the two on the
Cotton Trade during and after the Napoleonic Wars,
read by Professor Daniels.[4]   For economic historians
they have a unique value.

Of the post-war years suffice it to say that the range
of subjects and the quality of the contributions have
been worthy of the traditions of the Society.   Economists
and statisticians of our own household, like Professors
Flux, Macgregor, Daniels, Clay, and Gregory, have
given some of their best work.   Papers have been read
by historians like the late Professor Unwin and Dr.
Redford.   We have had distinguished visitors, like
Sir William Beveridge, Sir George Paish, Sir Henry
Maybury, and R. G. Hawtrey.   Politicians, like Arthur
Greenwood, P. M. Oliver, and Austin Hopkinson, have
appeared before us; men of affairs, like Sir Ernest Simon
and F. J. Marquis; and public servants, like Harold
Butler and John Hilton.   It may be that some author of
a paper feels that his name has been wrongly omitted
from these pages, or that insufficient attention has been
paid to his discoveries.   If so, let him hope that repara-
tion will be made by that member, yet unborn, to whom
the Council will entrust the task of writing a fuller and
better history than this, on the occasion of the Bicentenary
of the Society, in the year of our Lord 2,033.

[1] " A Problem of After-War Reconstruction—The Study of Foreign
Languages," March 1919.
[2] " The British Mercantile Marine in its Relation in the Past to the
State," February 1918.
[3] " The Future of British Railways," December 1918.
[4] " The Effect of the Napoleonic War on the Cotton Trade," Session
1915–16; " The Cotton Trade at the Close of the Napoleonic War,"
Session 1917–18.

CHAPTER XI

DOMESTIC AFFAIRS

THE *Transactions* are the face we show to the world. It remains to say something of internal structure and our progress as a living organism. The thirteen men who formed the Society in September 1833 were all personal friends: with the object of preserving the sociable character of the meetings, they determined that the ordinary membership should be limited to fifty. The annual subscription was fixed at one guinea; members were to be elected by ballot; and two black balls were to suffice to exclude a nominee. Benjamin Heywood was elected President, Lieutenant-Colonel Shaw-Kennedy and John Kennedy became Vice-Presidents, and Dr. Kay Treasurer. Though there is no record of the fact in the first session, it is likely that the detailed work of the Society fell to W. R. Greg and William Langton; and when a list of officers was published, along with the Rules, on November 19, 1834, Greg was serving as Corresponding Secretary and Langton as Minute Secretary. It is to the meticulous care of these men in preserving the letters and other manuscripts that we owe our knowledge of the first seven years of the history of the Society.[1]

Restricted membership is not without drawbacks. In order to avoid the danger of parochialism not only were " strangers " admitted as occasional visitors, but " gentlemen distinguished for their ability and zeal in cultivating Statistical inquiries, and living at least ten miles distant from Manchester " might be elected as Corresponding

[1] They are contained in a large Guard Book in the Manchester Reference Library.

members, without fee.[1]   At the end of the first session the Corresponding members numbered six.   The
nomination of the Rev. Thomas Chalmers, Professor of
Divinity in the University of Edinburgh, was probably
an act of piety on the part of Dr. Kay and the Gregs, who
had studied in Edinburgh ; that of Principal Macfarlane
of the University of Glasgow represented a tribute of
Benjamin Heywood to his *alma mater*.   The others were
Dr. Cleland (Superintendent of Public Works for
Glasgow and afterwards President of the Glasgow and
Clydesdale Statistical Society), William Kerr Ewart, of
Bombay, and David Henry Levyssohn, Advocate of the
Hague (relatives of two ordinary members of the Society)
and Sir Oswald Mosley.   In the session 1836–7, the
names of a distinguished public servant, Leonard Horner,
and of Dr. Kay (then Assistant Poor Law Commissioner
in East Anglia) were added ; and in the list of the following year appears the name of G. R. Porter.

By the second meeting, on October 16, 1833, the
membership had grown to eighteen, and by the end of
the first session to twenty-eight.   But twenty-eight
guineas would not go very far towards meeting the
expenses of the social inquiries that had been set on foot.
It had become clear that, if the usefulness of the Society
were not to be crippled, its income must be increased.
A sub-committee appointed at the Annual Meeting felt
unable to pronounce on the best way of effecting this end,
and contented itself with pointing out the alternatives.
The Society might continue as a group of friends,
meeting more or less informally ; but, in this case, it
would be necessary to raise additional funds by voluntary
subscriptions.   Or it might follow the London Statistical
Society in setting no bound to the number of members,
and appointing a Council for executive purposes.   A
general meeting held at Claremont, the house of Benjamin Heywood, on October 15, 1833, resolved that a
sufficient sum having been subscribed to enable the
Society to continue its inquiries during the ensuing year,

---

[1] *Rules of the Manchester Statistical Society*, November 19, 1834.

no alteration should be made in the constitution. A month later, however, when the rules were drawn up, the annual subscription was raised to two guineas; and in 1837 the rule that limited the number of ordinary members to fifty was rescinded. Nevertheless, a large part—probably the greater part—of the revenue came from donations of members like Benjamin and James Heywood and the McConnels.

The early meetings were held at the homes of the Heywoods, Dr. Kay, William Langton, or some other member; but in January 1835 a soirée took place at the York Hotel; and in 1839 the annual meeting made use of the rooms of the Chamber of Commerce. By 1840, when the membership had reached sixty, an official, James Orme, had been appointed to collect the subscriptions: he was remunerated by a commission of $2\frac{1}{2}$ per cent. of the sums brought in. Possibly we may infer from the following item in his bill that, by this time, the Society had secured premises of its own:

Dr. To providing Tea, Coffee &c. including Candles and Mrs. Orme's Attendance, 8 meetings . . . £4 10s.

But the first definite reference to a permanent home is in the *Transactions* for the session 1855–6, which shows that rooms had been obtained at 14, Ridgefield, John Dalton Street.

During its early years the Society maintained close contact with other learned bodies. It was as the result of a recommendation made at the Cambridge Meeting of the British Association in 1833 that the Manchester and London Statistical Societies had been brought into being. In the following year Benjamin Heywood gave the results of his inquiry into a selected area of working-class Manchester before the Statistical Section of the British Association at Edinburgh. In 1835, when five of our members attended the Dublin meeting to read papers, the Rev. Edward Stanley was made Vice-President of the Section (under Charles Babbage), W. R. Greg became one of its secretaries, and William

Langton was appointed to the Committee. Several grants were made by the British Association towards the cost of prosecuting the inquiries of the Society into education and working-class conditions.[1]   And in 1837 (when James Heywood served as Vice-President, and William Langton and W. R. Greg as Secretaries, of the Section) it was resolved that the Statistical Societies of Manchester and London should each enjoy the privilege of sending three deputies to the General Committee.

With the Statistical Society of London relations were no less cordial.   When its Provisional Committee issued a prospectus in April 1834, it expressed the hope of seeing " local societies springing up in every part of the British dominions, in direct and constant connection with the London Society, circulating its queries in their immediate neighbourhood, and collecting and authenticating the answers."   A month later, its Secretary, E. C. Tufnell, wrote asking for an outline of the proceedings of the Manchester group, and for copies of any reports they might have printed.[2]   The association thus established brought benefit to both parties.   Benjamin and James Heywood became Life-Fellows of the London Society.   The Manchester statisticians supplied those of London with a list of the varied associations for the promotion of Literature and Science in Manchester. The first pages of the first number of the *Proceedings of the Statistical Society of London* were occupied with the inquiry into the condition of the working classes in the St. Michael's and New Cross wards of Manchester ; and later numbers contained contributions by Edward Stanley and James Heywood.   Of the social surveys of the northerners the *Journal* of the London Society spoke in terms of high praise :

" The fact of this Society having, within the space of four years,

---

[1] For example, £50 was voted to help to defray the expenses of the investigation into the condition of the working classes in Manchester and the surrounding towns; and two other sums of £50 were given to meet the cost of the inquiries in Rutland.

[2] Letter in Guard Book, f. 9.

and with a permanent income of little more than £100 a year, completed seven extensive original enquiries, some of which have been prosecuted in distant towns, shews with what zeal its members have been animated, and affords both an example and an encouragement to similar societies in other places." [1]

And G. R. Porter remarked that " it was mainly owing to the publication of these results that the Statistical Society of London undertook similar investigations in various parts of the metropolis." [2]

Contact was maintained also with the other provincial societies, and publications were received from such social investigators as Dr. Cleland of Glasgow and William Felkin of Nottingham. Report of what was being done in Manchester even crossed the Channel. During the second session, de Tocqueville, just rising to fame, paid a visit to the Society; and, perhaps as a result, Baron Charles Dupin, Président de l'Academie Royale des Sciences, and M. Moreau de Jonnès, of the Statistical Department of the French Ministry of Commerce, presented copies of some of their works. In 1837 a letter was received from Charles Ross suggesting that the Society might publish its proceedings in his *Statistical Journal and Record of Useful Knowledge*; and in the same year a prospectus came from Palermo in Sicily relating to a projected *Giornale Di Statistica*. To the invitation from Ross, W. R. Greg replied that the Society would be willing to let him have its miscellaneous statistical papers; but its more elaborate reports would be published separately, " as the correction of the Press requires a degree of minute exactness and repeated revision which we could not delegate to other hands." [3] Several of the larger reports had already been printed, and in 1838 a collection of miscellaneous papers was issued.

After that for the session 1839–40 no annual report was preserved for several years. From what has already been said it is evident that in the early forties much

[1] *Journal of the Statistical Society of London*, Vol. I, p. 49.
[2] *Progress of the Nation*, p. 702.
[3] Letter of December 2, 1837. Guard Book, f. 102.

valuable research was accomplished. But towards the
end of the decade the activities of members reached a
low ebb. For one thing, the men whose enthusiasm had
brought the Society into being had turned elsewhere.
Kay-Shuttleworth had gone to East Anglia and London ;
William Langton was becoming increasingly absorbed
in archæological studies ; Edward Stanley had removed
to Norwich ; and the Gregs, like many others, had
followed Richard Cobden into the field of political
propaganda. Whatever the cause, the attendances at
the meetings had become so small that in 1849 the
winding up of the Society was seriously debated. It was
a coroner who saved the necessity for an inquest. Edward
Herford, who served Manchester in that office, was a
follower of Toulmin Smith. He had, as we have seen,
an intense belief in the value of voluntary and local
institutions, and an equally intense hatred of the cen-
tralising tendencies represented by Edwin Chadwick.
He saw in the Statistical Society an organ of civic life
that should not be allowed to die ; and his work in
effecting a broadening of the constitution and an increase
of members deserves that we should keep him in memory.
" To a late President," said Dr. Aspland [1] of Herford,
" we are perhaps more deeply indebted than to any other,
as he, interposing at a critical time, with earnestness of
purpose, and clearness of legal apprehension, prevented
the dissolution of the Society and the dispersion of its
funds. He was rewarded by witnessing the accomplish-
ment of laborious and useful work which has guided and
determined much sanitary legislation for the city of
Manchester."

The same apathy seems to have settled on the sister
societies in other towns. For the annual report of the
London Society for 1846 remarks that

" The only publication during the past year by a provincial
Statistical Society is that of the Statistical Society of Manchester
' On the Demoralisation and Injuries Occasioned by Want of

[1] Inaugural Address, Session 1863-4.

Proper Regulations of Labourers Engaged in the Construction or Making of Railways '; and it is not without regret that the Council witnesses how ephemeral is the existence, or transitory the exertions, of the local Statistical Societies."

Evidently the political temperature of 1846 was hostile to the study of social arithmetic. In this year the membership of our Society appears to have fallen to twenty-four ; but Herford managed to enlist sixteen recruits. Four years later the Council of the London Society referred to Manchester as

" a quarter to which the Council always looks with great interest as that which contains the first Statistical Society ever founded in Britain, and the only one which yet survives beyond the limit of the Metropolis. It is with pleasure that they have to announce its renewed activity on a more popular basis, and their hope that it will supply results worthy of notice in your *Journal*." [1]

The more popular basis consisted of the lowering of the annual subscription to half-a-guinea (with an admission fee also of half-a-guinea) and a slight change in the rule as to exclusion : whereas formerly two black balls had served to negative the election of a candidate, henceforth six were required. At the same time the Executive Committee was enlarged. Under the rules adopted in 1834 three ordinary members had been chosen at the annual meeting to serve with the officers : under the new rules of 1849–50 eight ordinary members were to be elected, and those who had passed the presidential chair were also added to the Committee. A minor change was also made in the period of office of the President. Formerly he had been appointed for a period not exceeding three years ; hereafter two successive years were the maximum period of office—until the session 1932–33, when (owing to circumstances connected with the approaching Centenary celebration) Professor G. W. Daniels was confirmed in the office of President for a third year. The improvement in its financial position made it possible for the Society to grant £10 towards the cost of publishing a

[1] *Annual Report*, 1849–50.

History of the Cholera in Manchester in 1849, by John Leigh (afterwards Medical Officer of Health for the city) and Ker Gardiner; and a few years after the reconstruction the publication of the *Transactions* was begun.

It has already been mentioned that the Crimean War, and the consequent interest in sanitary statistics, led many medical men to join the Society: in the session 1857–8 a Committee was appointed to collect statistical information from the Manchester Barracks and Military Hospitals. Lawyers also took a prominent part in the activities of this period. In his inaugural address of November 1857, Canon Richson announced the formation of a Juridical Section for the study of " the connection of law with the moral, social and political condition of the people "; and the proceedings of this group were opened by W. D. Lewis (who came from London for the purpose) in a paper " On Some Popular Errors concerning Law." During the following session papers on legal topics were read by such members as Thomas Potter, Dr. Noble, and G. H. Little; but, since no further reference is made to the section, we may infer that its life, as a separate entity, was not a long one.

The fifties were a time of rapid extension of the Society, and by 1861 the number of ordinary members had reached 144. The three succeeding years of the Cotton Famine saw a falling off to 116; but thereafter progress was steady, and in 1868 the ordinary members numbered 170. At the same time distinguished names began to appear among the Corresponding members. The famous Belgian statistician, Adolphe Quetelet, had long served in that capacity. In the session 1860–1 William Newmarch was added to the list, and in that of 1862–3 Frederick Purdy, Editor of the *Journal of the London Statistical Society*. In 1868–9 Dr. Engel, of the Statistical Department, Berlin, became a Corresponding member; and in the following session he was joined by Leone Levi of London, Adolphe Soetbeer of Hamburg, and Michael Chevalier and Louis Wolowski of Paris.

The growth of numbers made the premises at 14,Ridgefield inadequate; after the session 1865–6 these were given up, and subsequent meetings were held, either at the Clarence Hotel, or at the Memorial Hall in Albert Square. In December 1865, " with a view to promote co-operation and mutual good feeling between the two Statistical Societies of Manchester and London," the President, David Chadwick, entertained at dinner at the Queen's Hotel the present and past officers of both societies. Among those who attended were William Newmarch, William Farr, Frederick Purdy, and (of our founders) Samuel Greg, William Langton, John Roberton, and Samuel Robinson.

In local affairs there are many evidences of activity. In 1862–3 a Committee inquired into " the causes of the alleged diminished death rate in Lancashire "; and another into " the best means of obtaining *uniform* and reliable criminal statistics in this county." The following year the sum of £40 was granted to facilitate the inquiries into the educational and other conditions of the Deansgate and Ancoats areas; and in 1866–7 a sub-committee to inquire into the registration of deaths invited the co-operation of the London Statistical Society and the Manchester and Salford Sanitary Association. The result was a Memorial sent to the Home Secretary, urging compulsory powers to secure a scientific record of the causes of death, and the appointment of duly qualified Officers of Health. No reforms followed immediately. But in the session 1871–2 the Society prepared an amended form of death certificate, " filled up according to statistical nosology " to which the Registrar-General promised his consideration. It is not improbable that the adoption of compulsory civil registration of deaths, in 1875, owed something to the efforts of our Society.

Though the early seventies were, on the whole, a period of expansion of local trade, the membership dropped to 148 by the middle of the decade. It was, no doubt, this decline that led to a revision of the rules in 1875. The abolition of the entrance fee of half-a-guinea was followed by an immediate access of new members; and by 1879 the number on the roll had reached 214. In April 1876, the Council of the London Statistical Society paid us the compliment of resolving that the President for the time being of the Statistical Society of Manchester be elected an honorary Fellow of the Statistical Society of London; and in 1878–9 it presented the Manchester Society with eighty-four back numbers of its *Journal*. Additions to the corresponding membership of our Society during these years included Stephen Bourne and R. H. Inglis Palgrave, Professor Erben of Prague, Professor Josef Koroski of Buda Pesth, Dr. A. Chervin of Paris, and Signor L. Bodio of the Italian Ministry of Agriculture, Industry, and Commerce.

In 1871 the Executive Committee had decided to form a Library of works on Statistics and Political Economy, and W. E. A. Axon had undertaken the arrangement of the Society's books and papers. Two years later he purchased about ninety volumes of statistical works for the Library, and donations of books from members so added to the collection that the space available at the Memorial Hall was becoming insufficient. The Committee considered the possibility of co-operation with other Literary and Scientific Societies in the town with the object of finding a fitting home for its library. But this came to nothing; and in 1878 the books were transferred to the Reference Library, on the understanding that they could be consulted by the public and borrowed by members of the Society. A year earlier the Committee had sent a memorial to the City Council in favour of the transfer of the Reference Library to the Old Town Hall in King Street; it had urged on the Trustees of the British Museum the need of the publication of a list of additions to the national library; and it had petitioned the Privy Council in favour of granting to Owens College a charter of incorporation as a University.

The eighties were a period of active work in several directions. During the session 1881–2 the Society lost by death the last survivors of its founders in the persons of W. R. Greg and William Langton. In the same year

Gustav Behrens, who had joined the Society in 1875, was elected to the Council (which, under the revised rules of 1880, had replaced the Executive Committee). He still remains an honoured, if no longer an active, member of the Society. In 1886 the Council addressed to the Treasury a memorial in favour of the free distribution to public libraries of Parliamentary papers and blue-books; in 1887–8 it petitioned the Registrar-General to improve the registration of the causes of death; and it formed a local committee to assist the British Association in an investigation into " the effects of different occupations and employments on the physical development of the human body." In 1889, a deputation, headed by Professor Munro, urged on the Chancellor of the Exchequer the need for an improvement of the Census, especially in the matter of the returns of occupation and industry.

The trade depression of the early nineties was no doubt accountable for a fall of membership, from 185 in 1890 to 160 in 1894. In the session 1894–5, however, the Council issued a circular inviting " those gentlemen who were interested in questions of social and political economy " to join the Society, and the result was an access of sixty-one new members. Otherwise, the decade was marked by no events deserving mention; though in the year 1900 the Council addressed the House of Lords in favour of a quinquennial Census, and made suggestions for the classification of workers in the coal and cotton industries, which were adopted by the Registrar-General.

The opening of the twentieth century saw a further growth of membership, and in the session 1901–2 the numbers reached 219. At the same time the ranks of the Corresponding members were strengthened by the election of Professors Flux and Foxwell and of Sir Robert Giffen. In the pre-war years it was the practice of the Society to entertain at an annual dinner distinguished visitors, among whom were Earl Grey, Sir Edward Holden, and Sir William Plender. Earl Grey was responsible for

the Society's request to the School Board of Manchester
and Salford, in 1902, that they should keep a half-yearly
record of the weight and measurement of school-children ;
and such a record was taken at two schools.   In 1909–10
F. L. Pritchard and F. Vernon Hansford, to whom the
Society owes much, collected material in aid of the
investigation, conducted for the British Association by
Professor Bowley, into the size of the national income ;
and in 1914 it was reported that a paper read before the
Society had led to the setting up of a branch of the office
of the Public Trustee in Manchester.

From its high mark of 1902 the membership of the
Society declined to 170 in 1913–14 and to 142 in 1920.
The post-war years saw a revival, and in 1921–22 the
maximum of 227 was reached.   Continued local depression brought the figure down again to 170 in 1931–32 ;
but a growth of six was registered in the following session,
and this increase will, no doubt, be far exceeded in the
Centenary year.   Since the war the Society has found a
home befitting its traditions, among the phials and
crucibles of John Dalton, in the house of the Literary and
Philosophical Society in George Street.   There have been
many changes ; but the notices with which the Secretary
reminds members of approaching meetings still carry a
spice of early days—" Coffee on the table at 5.30 o'clock
precisely."   A new development, full of promise, is the
formation of a group for the study of statistical method ;
and under the presidency of an eminent scholar, the
Chancellor of the University, who contributes the Introduction to this volume, the Society enters on its second
century with confidence.

" Societies," remarked Dr. Hook,[1] once Vicar of
Leeds, " are from their constitution braggarts " ; and
though the stricture was passed on propagandist rather
than learned bodies, we must take heed.   Enough has
been shown of solid achievement to make it unnecessary

[1] Cited by J. L. and Barbara Hammond, *The Age of the Chartists*,
p. 202.

to close with a panegyric: let the last words be rather those of warning. The besetting danger of such associations as ours is that they should become debating societies, or mere amplifiers for the commonplaces of public men. Our business (in the worn phrase) is, not with figures of speech, but with figures of arithmetic. It is the deeper currents, rather than the surface movements of social life that we have to watch. Lancashire needs a statistical society to-day, as she needed one a hundred years ago. But if it is to perform its function of helping Lancashire to a knowledge of herself, our Society must be guided by men alert to distinguish what is permanently significant from what is only immediately striking. Perhaps a book made up so largely of quotations may end with one borrowed from the title-page of a work by a founder of the Society.[1] It has implications for our smaller community, no less than for the nation:

" *Mr. Pitt :* I have no fear for England: she will stand till the Day of Judgment.
" *Mr. Burke :* It is the day of *no* judgment that I dread."

[1] W. R. Greg, *Rocks Ahead, or the Warnings of Cassandra.*

APPENDIX A

THE MANCHESTER STATISTICAL SOCIETY
ESTABLISHED 1833

LIST OF PRESIDENTS

BENJAMIN HEYWOOD	1833–1834
LIEUT.-COL. SHAW-KENNEDY	1834–1836
REV. EDWARD STANLEY	1836–1837
THOMAS ASHTON	1837–1839
SHAKESPEARE PHILLIPS	1839–1840
WILLIAM LANGTON	1841–1844
JOHN ROBERTON	1844–1847
SAMUEL ROBINSON	1847–1849
HENRY HOULDSWORTH	1849–1850
WILLIAM NIELD	1850–1851
ROBT. N. PHILIPS	1851–1853
JAMES HEYWOOD	1853–1855
WILLIAM METCALF	1855–1857
REV. C. J. RICHSON	1857–1859
DANIEL NOBLE	1859–1861
EDWARD HERFORD	1861–1863
ALFRED ASPLAND	1863–1865
DAVID CHADWICK	1865–1867
WILLIAM LANGTON	1867–1869
WILLIAM STANLEY JEVONS	1869–1871
JOHN MILLS	1871–1873
JOHN WATTS	1873–1875
THOMAS READ WILKINSON	1875–1877
THOMAS DICKINS	1877–1879
ELIJAH HELM	1879–1881
HENRY BAKER	1881–1883
JOHN SLAGG	1883–1884
ROBERT MONTGOMERY	1884–1886
THOS. B. MOXON	1886–1888
EDWIN GUTHRIE	1888–1890
J. E. C. MUNRO	1890–1892
WILLIAM FOGG	1892–1894
W. H. S. WATTS	1894–1896
GEORGE H. POWNALL	1896–1898

Right Rev. L. C. Casartelli	1898–1900
Professor A. W. Flux	1900–1901
Sir W. H. Houldsworth, Bart.	1901–1903
Fredk. Merttens	1903–1905
Fredk. Brocklehurst	1905–1907
James Niven	1907–1909
Professor S. J. Chapman	1909–1911
Sir Drummond Fraser	1911–1913
Theodore Gregory	1913–1915
Barnard Ellinger	1915–1917
Very Rev. Mgr. Anselm Poock	1917–1919
Sir Christopher T. Needham	1919–1921
Frank Roby	1921–1923
Professor Henry Clay	1923–1925
W. H. Goulty	1925–1927
Sir William Clare Lees	1928–1929
Sir Kenneth D. Stewart	1929–1930
Professor G. W. Daniels	1930–1933
The Right Hon. the Earl of Crawford and Balcarres	1933–1934

APPENDIX B

Membership of the Society.

End of Session	Number	End of Session	Number
1833–4	28	1891–2	168
1834–5	40	1892–3	166
1835–6	46	1893–4	160
1836–7	52	1894–5	199
1837–8	60	1895–6	200
1838–9	58	1896–7	203
1839–40	60	1897–8	197
		1898–9	203
		1899–1900	208
1857–8	119	1900–1	209
1858–9	135	1901–2	219
1859–60	137	1902–3	204
1860–1	144	1903–4	207
1861–2	128	1904–5	205
1862–3	116	1905–6	191
1863–4	124	1906–7	183
1864–5	131	1907–8	180
1865–6	162	1908–9	174
1866–7	166	1909–10	174
1867–8	170	1910–11	171
1868–9	157	1911–12	171
1869–70	143	1912–13	177
1870–1	159	1913–14	170
1871–2	160	1914–15	161
1872–3	155	1915–16	153
1873–4	144	1916–17	149
1874–5	148	1917–18	143
1875–6	163	1918–19	144
1876–7	178	1919–20	142
1877–8	198	1920–1	226
1878–9	214	1921–2	227
1879–80	208	1922–3	211
1880–1	206	1923–4	225
1881–2	205	1924–5	222
1882–3	201	1925–6	198
1883–4	198	1926–7	204
1884–5	193	1927–8	192
1885–6	188	1928–9	187
1886–7	183	1929–30	188
1887–8	173	1930–1	172
1888–9	181	1931–2	170
1889–90	185	1932–3	176
1890–1	180		

APPENDIX C

List of Reports and Papers

The mark x denotes that no copy has been preserved by the Society.
m denotes manuscript only.

REPORTS

m On the Number of Sunday Schools in Manchester and Salford. (1834.)
m On 4,102 Families of Working Men in Manchester. (1834.)
m On the Associations for the Promotion of Literature and Science in
   Manchester. (1834.)
m A Survey of Irlams-o'-th'-Height. (1835.)
m On Immoral and Irreligious Works Sold in Manchester. (1835.)
   On the State of Education in Manchester in 1834. (1835.)
   On the State of Education in Bury. (1835.)
m On the Means of Religious Instruction in Manchester and Salford.
   (1836.)
   On the State of Education in Salford in 1835. (1836.)
m On the Parish of Alderley. (1836.)
   On the State of Education in Liverpool in 1835–36. (1836.)
   On the Use of Steam Power in Manchester and Salford. (1837.)
   On the Use of Steam Power in Bolton. (1837.)
   On the State of Education in Bolton. (1837.)
m On the Quantity of Meat Consumed in Manchester and Salford in
   1836. (1837.)
   On the Quantity of Coal Brought into Manchester in 1834 and 1836.
   (1837.)
   On the State of Education in York, 1836–37. (1837.)
   On the Condition of the Working Classes in an Extensive Manufacturing
   District in 1834, 1835, and 1836. (1838.)
   On the State of Education in Pendleton, 1838. (1839.)
   On the Condition of the Population in Three Parishes in Rutlandshire.
   (1839.)
   On the State of Education in the County of Rutland in the year 1838.
   (1839.)
   On the State of Education in Kingston-upon-Hull. (1840.)
   On the Condition of the Working Classes of Kingston-upon-Hull.
   (1841.)
   On the Educational and other Conditions of a District in Deansgate.
   (1864.)

On the Educational and other Conditions of a District in Ancoats.
(1865.)
On the Defects of the System of Registration of Deaths.   (1867.)
On an Amended Form of Death Certificate.   (1871.)

PAPERS

Session 1833–34

M A Brief Memoir on the Present State of Criminal Statistics. *W. R. Greg.*
x Plans and Estimates for Public Swimming Baths for the Use of the Operative Population. *Dr. J. P. Kay.*
x The Present State of Education in this and Other Countries. *S. Greg.*
On the Defects of the Present Constitution of Dispensaries. *Dr. J. P. Kay.*
M Result of a Conference with Mr. Thomson concerning the Objects towards which the Society should direct its Attention. *Dr. J. P. Kay.*
Analysis of the Evidence taken before the Factory Commissioners as far as it relates to the Population of Manchester and the Vicinity engaged in the Cotton Trade. *S. and W. R. Greg.*
x On the Condition of the Miners in Derbyshire. *Dr. J. P. Kay.*
M Abstract of Answers and Returns under the Population Act 11 Geo. IV, c. 30, Enumeration 1831, relating to Manchester. *W. Langton.*

Session 1834–35

x The Means Existing for the Religious Instruction of the Working Classes in Large Towns. *Dr. J. P. Kay.*
M Tables Showing the Number of Churches, Chapels and Sunday Schools in Manchester and District. *W. Langton.*
M Tables Showing the Total Number of Felons Committed to the New Bailey, Salford, 1809–27. *Rev. H. Fielding.*
M Tables Showing the Number of Churches and Chapels of Ease in each County compared with the Population. *W. R. Greg.*
M Inquiry into the State of the Population of Irlams-o'-th'-Height. *B. Heywood.*
M Report on the Associations for the Promotion of Literature and Science in Manchester. *B. Heywood.*
M On the Classification of Offences. *H. Romilly.*
Comparative View of the Business Transacted in the Court of Requests and the Court Baron, showing the Comparative Expenses in each Court. *S. D. Darbishire.*
M Education and Religious State of Alderley. *Rev. E. Stanley.*

Session 1835–36

M Economical Statistics of the Parish of Birmingham. *S. Beale.*
M Statistical Report on the Parish of Alderley. *Rev. E. Stanley.*

x Proposed Plan of a University or College in Manchester. *Rev. H. L. Jones.*

Session 1836–37

M The State of the Brussels and Antwerp Railway. *G. Loch.*

M Returns from Marylebone, London and from Seven Parishes in Kent on the Condition of the Poor. *M. Duppa.*

M Number of Steam Engines and Water Wheels in the Bolton District. *H. & E. Ashworth.*

M State of Employment of a Considerable Number of People in Ancoats. *W. Langton.*

Employed and Unemployed Steam and Water Power in Manchester and Chorlton-on-Medlock. *W. Langton.*

M Ardwick Sick and Burial Society. *Rev. W. W. Gibson.*

x The State of Education in York in 1826, the result of an enquiry carried out by the Society of Friends ; also a Classification of the books kept at the Retreat (Lunatic Asylum), York. *J. R. Wood.*

x Account of the Institutions of M. de Fellenberg at Hofwyl. *J. R. Wood.*

Account of the Turn-out in Preston, October, 1836. *H. Ashworth.*

Session 1837–38

M Statistical Desiderata. *W. R. Greg.*

M Report of the Probable Annual Consumption of Butcher's Meat in Manchester, 1836. *W. McConnel.*

M Report on the Quantity of Coal brought into Manchester in 1834. *J. Meadows.*

M Notes on Criminal Statistics. *S. Greg.*

x Medical Statistics. *S. Greg.*

M Attendance at Places of Worship in York. *J. R. Wood.*

x Particulars Relative to the Education and Domestic Comforts of 175 Families Living in Miles Platting. *J. Heywood.*

x On National Education. *W. R. Greg.*

x On the Past and Present Numbers of Aborigines in the British Colonies. *P. M. James.*

Session 1838–39

M Savings Banks in France. *Rev. H. L. Jones.*

M Popular Education in France. *F. E. Wembergue.*

x The Handloom Weavers in Miles Platting. *W. Langton.*

x Preliminary Report on the State of Education in Macclesfield. *S. Greg.*

x State of Some of the Fine Spinning Mills in Manchester in 1832. *J. Shuttleworth.*

M Consumption of Food Stuffs in Lyons. *Rev. H. L. Jones.*

M Number of Sunday Schools in Dukinfield. *S. Robinson.*

Session 1839-40

x Statistics of Two Schools in one of the Most Populous Districts in Manchester. *Rev. J. J. Taylor.*

x On the Large Proportion of Indigent and Improvident Families in Manchester, as shown by the Returns of the Lying-In Hospital. *J. Roberton.*

x The Abuses of Medical Charities. *W. Langton.*

x Numbers of the Various Religious Denominations in Hull. *W. Langton.*

x Condition of the Population in St. James' and St. Margaret's, Westminster. *J. Heywood.*

x The Relative Proportion of Male and Female Population. *J. Roberton.*

Session 1840-41

м Some Statistical Details Respecting the State of Schools in Larne in Ireland. *J. Heywood.*

x Remarks on a Proposal to Withhold Outdoor Relief from Widows with Families contained in the last Report of the Poor Law Commissioners for England and Wales. *J. Roberton.*

x Report on the State of Education in Trinity College and other Colleges of the University of Cambridge. *J. Heywood.*

x Summary of Report of the Committee on the Condition of the Working Classes in Hull, as shown by Mr. J. R. Wood's Returns. *W. Langton.*

Session 1841-42

x Report on the System of Education in France. *Rev. H. L. Jones.*

x Report on the Treatment of Juvenile Offenders in the New Bailey Prison. *E. Herford.*

x On the Change in the Rate of Mortality in England. *W. R. Greg.*

x On the Present State of Trade and Commerce in France. *Rev. H. L. Jones.*

x On a Branch of Medical Statistics Connected with the Natural History of the Negro Race. *J. Roberton.*

x Abstract of the Baptisms, Marriages, and Burials in the Collegiate Church, Manchester, at certain periods since the year 1575. *W. Langton.*

x Report on the Geology of the Town and Neighbourhood of Manchester. *E. W. Binney.*

x Preface to the Report of the Registration Committee. *J. Roberton.*

Session 1842-43

x On the Medical Inspection of Towns and the Registration of the Causes of Death. *P. H. Holland.*

x Early Marriages in Oriental Countries as Evidence of Early Puberty. *J. Roberton.*

Session 1843-44

x Report from the Committee for the Registration of Births, Deaths, and Marriages. *J. Roberton.*
x On the Alleged Influence of Climate on Female Puberty in Greece. *J. Roberton.*

Session 1844-45

x On Certain Alleged Effects of Climate on Man. *J. Roberton.*
x On the Physiology of the Hindoos. *J. Roberton.*

Session 1845-46

x On Some of the Evils Affecting the Labourers Engaged in Railway Construction. *J. Roberton.*
x Descriptive Remarks Relating to Railway Contracts and Railway Workmen. *R. Rawlinson.*
x Memoranda on Facts and Suggestions in Respect of Measures for the Prevention of the Evils Attendant on the Want of Regulations as to the Mode of Employing and Paying Labourers on Railways. *E. Chadwick.*

Session 1846-47

No Record.

Session 1847-48

x On the Alleged Influence of Poverty in Accelerating the Increase of Population. *J. Roberton.*
x On Agricultural Statistics. *C. Lamport.*
x On the Amount of Capital Sunk in the Formation of a Railway, and its Effects on the Currency. *C. Lamport.*

Session 1848-49

No Record.

Session 1849-50

x On the Best Means of Improving the Climate of Manchester. *J. Roberton.*
x On the Mortality from Burns and Scalds, especially among the Children of the Labouring Poor. *S. Crompton.*
x On Medical Relief to the Sick and Destitute Poor. *Dr. D. Noble.*

Session 1850-51

x Money, and the Circumstances which Determine its Value. *T. H. Williams.*

L

Session 1851-52

x Some Statistical Tables of Vagrancy in South Lancashire, with Remarks thereon. *Capt. Sheppard.*

x Some Observations on the Subject of Vagrants, their Habitations and Modes of Life in Manchester. —. *Gifford.*

x On Land Tenures and their Influence upon the Cultivation of the Soil, the Employment of Labour, the Profitable Use of Drainage, etc. *J. Roberton.*

Are the Laws and Customs of England, which interfere with the Partition of Landed Property amongst Children, and with the Free Disposal of it as a Marketable Commodity, Beneficial or Injurious to Society ? *J. Roberton.*

Session 1852-53

x On Certain Misconceptions of the Law of Supply and Demand, which are to be found in the Discussions now going on as to the Effect of an Increase of Quantity upon the Value of Gold. *T. H. Williams.*

x On the Probable Effects of the Australian Discoveries on the Future of the Competing Classes at Home. *W. Medcalf.*

x On the Nurture and Training of Children in England and Germany. *J. Kay.*

x On University Education. *J. Heywood.*

x On the Progress and Results of the Present System of Providing Education for the Humbler Classes in Manchester. *W. R. Callender, Jun.*

x An Account of the Glasgow Refuges for Male and Female Criminals. *J. Roberton.*

x Suggestions for the Improvement of Municipal Government in Populous Manufacturing Towns. *J. Roberton.*

x On Quarantine Regulations. *A. Aspland.*

Session 1853-54

On the Fallacies Involved in Certain " Returns of the Number of Day Schools and Day Scholars in England and Wales, in 1818, 1833, and 1851," ordered by the House of Commons to be printed 13th May, 1853. *Rev. C. Richson.*

On the Municipal Institutions of the City of Manchester. *W. Medcalf.*

On Some Fallacies of Political Economy. *E. Herford.*

On Emigration ; and its Effects on Commerce. *J. Dunn.*

Suggestions for the Improvement of Municipal Government in Populous Manufacturing Towns. *J. Roberton.*

On Baths and Wash-houses for the People. *E. T. Bellhouse.*

Session 1854-55

On the Daily Education of Pauper Children. *Rev. Canon Richson.*

On the Advantages of the University of Oxford. *J. Heywood.*

An Account of the Educational Charity founded by William Hulme, formerly of Kearsley, near Bolton-le-Moors. *A. Kay.*

On the Malays of Cape Town. *J. W. Mayson.*
On the National Schools of Ireland. *J. Roberton.*
On the Diet of the Poor, in connection with the Tenure of Landed
Property. —. *Paterson.*

Session 1855–56

On the Agencies and Organisation Required in a National System of
Education. *Rev. Canon Richson.*
On Cambridge Academical Statistics. *J. Heywood.*
On Juvenile Criminals, Reformatories, and the Means of Rendering
the Perishing and Dangerous Classes Serviceable to the State.
J. Adshead.
On Some of the Vices of the Poor Law Medical Relief System.
D. Noble.
On the Defects, with reference to the Plan of Construction and
Ventilation, of most of our Hospitals for the Reception of the Sick
and Wounded. *J. Roberton.*
On Municipal Government. *W. Medcalf.*

Session 1856–57

On Certain Legalised Forms of Temptation as Causes of Crime.
J. Roberton.
On Some Economical Views of the Greek Philosophers. *Professor R. C.
Christie.*
On Certain Fallacies in our National Mortuary Returns. *A. Aspland.*
On National Education in Denmark. *E. Hald,* assisted by *M.
Kreiberg.*

Session 1857–58

On the Importance of Statistical and Economical Enquiries. *Rev.
Charles Richson.*
Observations on a Table Showing the Balance of Account between the
Mercantile Public and the Bank of England. *W. Langton.*
Additional Suggestions, with a View to the Improvement of Hospitals
for the Sick and Wounded. *J. Roberton.*
Observations on Money, Credit, and Panics. *T. R. Williams.*
x An Examination of the Prevailing Opinions as to the State of Crime in
England. *W. Medcalf.*
x On the Banda Oriental. *E. T. Bellhouse.*
x The Crisis of 1857; its Causes and Results. *W. R. Callender, Jun.*
x On Some Popular Errors Concerning Law. *W. D. Lewis.*

Session 1858–59

First Steps to the Introduction of a System of Decimal Coinage. *Rev.
Canon Richson.*
On the Constitution and Functions of the Coroner's Court. *Daniel
Noble.*

The Insalubrity of the deep Cornish Mines, and as a Consequence the Physical Degeneracy and Early Deaths of the Mining Population. *J. Roberton.*

Suggestions for the More Effectual Prevention of Small Pox. *S. Crompton.*

An Examination of the Report of the Commissioners to Enquire into the Mortality of the Army. *A. Aspland.*

On Jurisprudence in its Relations to Commerce. *T. Potter.*

The Cost to the Government of Law and Justice in England, Ireland, and Scotland. *Rev. J. W. Watkin.*

x A Commercial Review of 1858. *T. H. Williams.*

x Novel Applications of the Principle of Assurance. *W. T. Hannam.*

x A Plan for the General Index of Parish Registers. *S. Service.*

x On the Relation between Local Authorities and Central Boards. *J. W. Hampson.*

x On the Successive Changes in the Constitution of the Court of Bankruptcy, and their Practical Effect. *G. H. Little.*

Session 1859–60

On Certain Popular Fallacies concerning the Production of Epidemic Diseases. *D. Noble.*

On the Union with Scotland. *Rev. J. W. Watkin.*

The Union with Ireland—its Social Aspects. *M. Fitzgerald.*

A Model Warehouse. *J. Roberton.*

Hints on Life Insurance. *A. Aspland.*

On the Bullion Reserve of the Bank of England. *W. Hooley.*

Life Assurance and Investment. *W. Hannam.*

x The Future of India. *G. H. Little.*

Session 1860–61

On the Need of Additional as well as Improved Hospital Accommodation for Surgical Patients in Manufacturing and Mining Districts, but especially in Manchester. *J. Roberton.*

A Plea for the Establishment of a Convalescent Hospital for Manchester and its Surrounding Districts. *J. Adshead.*

On the Statistics of Paris, and the Mode of Obtaining Facts for Mortuary Tables. *A. Aspland.*

On the Best Means of Obtaining and Recording the Vital Statistics of Towns with a View to the Prompt Application by the Local Authorities of Practical Sanitary Remedies. *D. Chadwick.*

Homes for the Working Classes. *G. Greaves.*

Some Further Remarks on the Homes of the Poor, and the Means of Improving their Condition. *T. Worthington.*

x On the Substitution of the Science of Wealth for the True Science of Political and Social Economy. *E. Herford.*

Session 1861–62

On the Social and Educational Statistics of Manchester and Salford. *D. Chadwick.*

On the Politico-Economic Results of Slavery in the Southern States of North America. *C. J. Herford.*

On the Laws of Nature's Ventilation, and their Application in the Construction of Dwellings, Schools, and Public Buildings. *J. Roberton.*

On Middle-Class Education. *T. Browning.*

x On Certain Important Economic Questions. *E. Herford.*

x On the Bonus System adopted by Life Assurance Companies, and the Propriety of their Revision or Abolition. *W. T. Hannam.*

Session 1862–63

Observations on Some of the Causes of Infanticide. *G. Greaves.*

Our Unemployed Females, and what may best be done with them. *Rev. A. Munro.*

Our Reformatories, and what we know of them. *A. Aspland.*

Our Criminal Legislation in Recent Years, and its Relation to the Alleged Increase of Crime in the Manufacturing Districts of Lancashire. *J. Berry Torr.*

x The Relief Afforded during the Present Distress. *G. M. Harrison.*

Session 1863–64

Inaugural Address at the Opening of Session 1863–64. *A. Aspland.*

Fluctuations in the Death Rate. *D. Noble.*

On the Laws referring to Child Murder and Criminal Abortion, with Suggestions for their Amendment. *G. Greaves.*

x On the Growth of Cotton and its Manufacture. *J. Ogden.*

x On Mining and Miners in the Erewash Valley. *W. Medcalf.*

x On Working Men's Comforts. *D. Machaffie.*

Session 1864–65

Inquiry into the Educational and other Conditions of a District in Deansgate. *H. C. Oats.*

On American Prisons. *A. Aspland.*

On the Principles and Practice of Municipal Institutions in England. *E. Herford.*

On the Alleged Depreciation of Gold. *T. Browning.*

The Duty of England to Provide a Gratuitous Compulsory Education for the Children of her Poorer Classes. *J. Roberton.*

The Social Condition of the Poorer Classes. *T. Dickins.*

Session 1865–66

Inquiry into the Educational and other Conditions of a District in Ancoats. *H. C. Oats.*

Thoughts on the Value and Significance of Statistics. *D. Noble.*
Our Sewer Rivers. *G. Greaves.*
The Education of the Lower Classes of the People, with some Remarks
on the Measures Proposed for Manchester and Salford, 1851.
S. Robinson.
Local Courts and Tribunals of Commerce. *R. M. Pankhurst.*
On the Audit of Public Accounts. *W. Rees.*

Session 1866–67

On the Value of Life Tables, National and Local, as Evidence of Sani-
tary Condition. *Dr. H. W. Rumsey.*
Some Account of the Pavilion Hospital recently Erected at the Chorlton
Union Workhouse, Withington, near Manchester. *T. Worthington.*
On the Social Statistics of Certain Boroughs and Townships in Lanca-
shire and Cheshire, during the last Twenty Years. *H. C. Oats.*
On Capital Punishments. *A. Aspland.*
On the Analogy between the Post Office, Telegraphs, and other Systems
of Conveyance of the United Kingdom, as regards Government
Control. *Professor W. S. Jevons.*

Session 1867–68

Introductory Observations on the Labours and Policy of the Society.
W. Langton.
On Credit Cycles, and the Origin of Commercial Crises. *J. Mills.*
On Industrial Schools, in Relation to the Education of the Country.
A. Aspland.
Report upon the Educational and other Conditions of a District at
Gaythorn and Knott Mill, Manchester, visited in January, 1868, with
Observations suggested by the Visitation. *T. R. Wilkinson.*
On the International Monetary Convention, and the Introduction of
an International Currency into this Kingdom. *Professor W. S.
Jevons.*
On Some Questions of Currency and Finance. *E. Herford.*

Session 1868–69

On the Prevention of Excessive Infant Mortality. *Mrs. M. A. Baines.*
On the Exemption of Private Property at Sea from Capture during
War. *R. M. Pankhurst.*
On the Licensing Laws, and Proposals for their Amendment. *Rev. S. A.
Steinthal.*
On Vagrants and Tramps. *T. B. L. Baker.*
x A Review of a Paper read by Mr. E. Herford on 13th March, 1867.
W. Langton.
x A Criticism on the Paper read by Dr. Pankhurst " On the Exemption
of Private Property at Sea from Capture during War." *Mrs. M.
Hamlin.*

A Review of the Cotton Trade of the United Kingdom during Seven Years, 1862–1868. *E. Helm.*

On Hulme's Educational Charity. *Reprint of a Paper read in 1855 by A. Kay.*

On Hulme's Educational Charity. *W. L. Dickinson.*

Session 1869–70

Inaugural Address on the Work of the Society in Connection with the Questions of the Day. *Professor W. S. Jevons.*

Observations on Combined Religious and Secular Instruction, and on the so-called " Religious Difficulty." *S. Robinson.*

On the Principle of Compulsion in Primary Education. *J. A. Bremner.*

Some Population Statistics for Sanitary Organisation. *Dr. Rumsey.*

Our Export Trade in Cotton Goods to India. *J. C. Ollerenshaw.*

x On the Best and Cheapest Modes of Recording Votes at Elections. *L. Aspland.*

Session 1870–71

On University Endowments and the Higher Education of the Nation. *Professor A. S. Wilkins.*

Certain Industrial and Social Aspects of England during the Fourteenth and Fifteenth Centuries. *Rev. R. H. Gibson.*

On the Comparative Mortality in Large Towns. *Dr. E. J. Syson.*

Observations on Infant Mortality, and the Death Rate in Large Towns. *T. R. Wilkinson.*

On Trades Unions in Relation to National Industry. *E. Helm.*

On the Post-Panic Period, 1866–70. *J. Mills.*

x On the Organisation of Societies, Nationally and Locally Considered. *R. Bailey Walker.*

Session 1871–72

Inaugural Address on the Scope and Method of Statistical Enquiry, and on some Questions of the Day. *J. Mills.*

On Certain Fallacies in Local Rates of Mortality. *Dr. Rumsey.*

On Some Published Results of the Census of 1871. *T. A. Welton.*

On Town Dwellings for the Working Classes. *G. T. Robinson.*

On the Growth of the Commercial Centre of Manchester, Movement of Population, and Pressure of Habitation—Census Decenniad 1861–71. *H. Baker.*

The Doctrine of Rent. *Professor Bonamy Price.*

x On the Waste of Wealth. *W. Hoyle.*

Session 1872–73

On Co-operation Considered as an Economic Element in Society. *Dr. J. Watts.*

On Ancient and Modern Luxury. *Professor A. S. Wilkins.*

On Medical Charities and their Abuses, with some Suggestions for their Reform. *W. O'Hanlon.*

On the Boarding-out System for the Training of Orphan Pauper Children. *C. J. Herford.*
Commercial Bank Diffusion in Provincial England, and its Relation to Population. *H. Baker.*

Session 1873–74

The Work of the First Manchester School Board. *Dr. J. Watts.*
The American Financial Crisis of 1873. *E. Helm.*
On Prison Discipline. *J. A. Bremner.*
On the Relative Proportion of the Sexes. *W. E. A. Axon.*
On Intemperance as a Factor in the Production of Diseases. *R. Martin.*

Session 1874–75

The Progress of the Mathematical Theory of Political Economy, with an Explanation of the Principles of the Theory. *Professor W. S. Jevons.*
Notes on the Movements of the Bank of England Reserve in the last Ten Years. *R. Montgomery.*
On Some Defects in the Statistics of Books and Libraries. *W. E. A. Axon.*
On the Facts of the Census (Vol. III). *R. B. Walker.*
Notes on the Relative Numbers of the Sexes amongst Emigrants, and on Kindred Topics. *T. A. Welton.*
Sanitary Progress, and its Obstacles in Manchester. *R. Martin.*
On the Pollution of Rivers and Water, and its Prevention. *J. C. Morrell.*
On the Proper Meaning of Certain Statistical Facts. *T. A. Welton.*
On Facts and Fictions of the Currency. *E. Herford.*
Statistics of the Deaf and Dumb. *W. E. A. Axon.*

Session 1875–76

On the Origin and History of the Manchester Statistical Society. Inaugural Address by the President. *T. R. Wilkinson.*
Notes on Elementary Education with Special Reference to the City of Manchester. *W. Hughes.*
On the English Census of Occupations, 1871 (two papers). *T. A. Welton.*
The Moral and Disciplinary Treatment of Prisoners. *T. Dickins.*
On the United Kingdom Alliance and its Prospects of Success. *Prof. W. S. Jevons.*
Some Comparisons between the Population of England in the Sixteenth and that in the Nineteenth Century. *Rev. R. H. Gibson.*
The Landowners of England and Wales. *W. Nuttall.*
The Prospects of the United Kingdom Alliance, with special reference to the Objections of Professor Jevons. *W. Hoyle.*
Remarks on Currency and Banking. *Sir Francis Hincks.*

Observations on a Continuation Table and Chart showing the " Balance of Account between the Mercantile Public and the Bank of England," 1844–75, with special reference to its course in the years 1866–75. *H. Baker.*

The Operation of the Poor Laws, with some suggestions for the Amendment thereof. *T. Chorlton.*

Appendix to *Transactions* :

Reprint of Mr. W. Langton's Paper on " Observations on a Table showing the Balance of Account between the Mercantile Public and the Bank of England," read December 30, 1857.

Reprint of a paper by Professor W. S. Jevons read before the London Statistical Society, April 17, 1866, " On the Frequent Autumnal Pressure in the Money Market, and the Action of the Bank of England."

Session 1876–77

On Coroners' Juries. *A. Hildebrandt.*

Banking Statistics as a Measure of Trade. *G. H. Pownall.*

On Alleged Defects in the Office of Coroner. *E. Herford.*

On the Influence of Note Circulation in the Conduct of Banking Business. *R. H. Inglis Palgrave.*

On the Increasing Dependence of this Country upon Foreign Supplies for Food. *S. Bourne.*

The Habitual Drunkards Bill. *S. Alford.*

Facts on Adult Education. *W. H. J. Traice.*

The Growth of the Cotton Trade in Great Britain, America, and the Continent of Europe, during the Half-century ending with the year 1875. *J. Spencer.*

On Baths and Wash-houses for the People in Manchester. *E. T. Bellhouse.*

Some Defects in the Statistics of the English Publishing Trade. *W. E. A. Axon.*

Session 1877–78

Inaugural Address by the President, on Social Conditions of the Time, and Discussion thereon. *T. Dickins.*

On Savings Banks, and Discussion thereon. *W. Langton.*

On the Recent Variation between the Bank and the Market Rates of Discount, and Discussion thereon. *T. B. Moxon.*

On English Prisons and the Prison Bill, and Discussion thereon. *Capt. R. A. Leggett.*

The Silver Question. *E. Helm.*

The Contagious Diseases of Cattle and their Influence on Meat Prices, with some Remarks on the Government Bill, and Discussion thereon. *J. Hyde.*

On Municipal Finance, and Discussion thereon. *J. Goodier.*

Session 1878–79

On the True Relation in which Imports and Exports should stand to each other in the Trade of a Prosperous Country. *S. Bourne.*
The Depression of Trade. *E. Helm.*
The Next Step in Primary Education. *Dr. J. Watts.*
The Cost of Administering the English Poor Law. *G. Rooke.*
Some Considerations Affecting the Relations of Capital and Labour. *G. H. Pownall.*
The Silver Question. *E. Langley.*
The Economical Aspects of the Land Question in England. *W. Summers.*
Statistical Notes on the Sunday Opening of Libraries and Museums. *W. E. A. Axon.*

Session 1879–80

The Revival of Trade : Inaugural Address by the President. *E. Helm.*
National Insurance, considered Economically and Practically. *Rev. W. L. Blackley.*
The Silver Controversy. *R. Montgomery.*
Stationary Populations. *T. A. Welton.*
The Border-land of Pauperism. *T. Dickins.*
The Economic Conditions of Good Trade. *W. Hoyle.*
The Coffee House Movement. *E. T. Bellhouse.*

Session 1880–81

The Decimal System as applied to Coinage, Weights and Measures. *E. Guthrie.*
The Treatment of Juvenile Offenders. *T. Dickins.*
Indian Finance. *T. B. Moxon.*
Poor Laws. *Rev. W. A. O'Connor.*
A Cheap and Compulsory Scheme for the Gradual Registration of Titles to Land. *T. Hewitt.*
Technical Industrial Education in Connection with Mechanics' Institutions and other Kindred Associations. *E. T. Bellhouse.*
Recent Savings Bank Legislation. *W. Langton.*

Session 1881–82

On the Growth of the Manchester Population, Extension of the Commercial Centre of the City, and Provision for Habitation, Census Period, 1871–81. *H. Baker.*
The Effects upon Trade of the Operation called " Cornering " in Relation to Commodities. *E. Guthrie.*
Deficient Harvest and Diminished Exports. *S. Bourne.*
Commercial Education. *Rev. L. C. Casartelli.*
A Patent Law. *W. H. J. Traice.*
On the Published Results of the Census of 1881. *T. A. Welton.*

On the Employment of Surplus Labour, more especially during Periods of Commercial Depression. *J. C. Fielden.*
Objections to Bimetallism Examined. *R. Barclay.*
The Cost of Theatrical Amusements. *W. E. A. Axon.*

Session 1882–83

Elementary Education in Manchester. *Dr. J. Watts.*
The Actual and Possible Cost of Conveyance between Manchester and Liverpool. *F. R. Condor.*
On the Near Approach of the Credit of Corporate Bodies to that of the State. *H. Baker.*
On Profit-sharing between Capital and Labour. *S. Taylor.*
Certain Statistics of New Zealand. *H. Gibson.*
Our Land Laws. *Rev. W. A. O'Connor.*
The Married Women's Property Act, 1882. *W. H. S. Watts.*
The Scarcity of Gold and the Remedy. *R. Montgomery.*
Education in Salford, Retrospective and Prospective. *W. E. A. Axon.*

Session 1883–84

On the Cost of Technical and Art Education in England and in Foreign Countries. *J. Slagg.*
The Land and the Nation. *Dr. Pankhurst.*
On the Revaluation by the State of the 3% Annuity on the National Debt. *H. Baker.*
Progress of Morals in England during the last Twenty-five Years. *Prof. Leone Levi.*
National Income and Expenditure. *T. B. Moxon.*
Certain Statistics of New Zealand (second paper). *R. H. Gibson.*

Session 1884–85

A Comparison of Some of the Economic and Social Conditions of Manchester and the surrounding Districts in 1834 and 1884. *R. Montgomery.*
Some Considerations on the Theory of Money. *Prof. R. Adamson.*
Local Taxation and Government. *G. H. Pownall.*
Proportional Representation. *L. Broderick.*
The Administration of Justice in Lancashire. *W. H. S. Watts.*
The Need for the Better Organisation of Benevolent Effort in Manchester and Salford. *F. Scott.*

Session 1885–86

Sliding Scales in the Iron Industry. *Prof. J. E. C. Munro.*
Work and Cost of the Manchester Corporation Health Department. *H. Whiley.*
One Aspect of Wealth Distribution. *Rev. W. A. O'Connor.*
Fifteen Years of School Board Work in Manchester. *Dr. John Watts.*

156   ECONOMIC AND SOCIAL INVESTIGATIONS

x On the Exchange and Distribution of the Products of Labour, and the
   Distribution of Wealth. *T. Illingworth.*
x On State Socialism and Individualism. *E. Guthrie.*

Session 1886–87
The Basis of Social Prosperity. *T. B. Moxon.*
The British Empire and Imperial Federation. *C. E. H. Vincent.*
Objections to Free Trade Answered. *W. Fogg.*
The Social Aspects of Co-operation. *E. Vansittart Neale.*
The Modern Science of Economics. *H. D. Macleod.*
Technical Education. *J. H. Reynolds.*

Session 1887–88
Socialism; its Argument and Aims. *Prof. W. Graham.*
The Prospects of International Arbitration. *R. M. Pankhurst.*
A Consideration of some of the Effects of the Landlords' Preferential
   Position upon Commerce and Agriculture. *R. C. Richards.*
Notes on Taxation and Rating. *T. H. Elliott.*
On the Vital Statistics of Towns. *Dr. A. Ransome.*
The Modern Languages Problem in Modern Education. *Rev. L. C.
   Casartelli.*
The Free Library Movement in Manchester. *W. R. Credland.*
The Constitution of the United States. *Hon. E. J. Hale.*

Session 1888–89
Inaugural Address by the President. *E. Guthrie.*
Colonisation. *Sir W. H. Houldsworth.*
Some Economic Aspects of Banking. *A. H. Cherry.*
Facts and Figures Relating to Street Children. *G. R. Kirlew.*
Elementary Education and the Act of 1870. *E. J. Broadfield.*
Some Phases of Technical Education. *Sir H. E. Roscoe.*
The Conditions and Occupations of the People of Manchester and
   Salford. *F. Scott.*

Session 1889–90
Local Government. *E. Guthrie.*
The Evidence of Statistics in Regard to our Social Condition. *J. R.
   Galloway.*
Home Colonisation. *Rev. H. V. Mills.*
Arbitration in Trade Disputes. *Dr. R. S. Watson.*
The Cost of our Drinking Customs. *J. Whyte.*
Manufacturing Processes in Relation to Health. *J. T. Arlidge.*
Statistics of the Colony of New Zealand for the year 1888.
   R. H. Gibson.

Session 1890–91
Our Bank-note System, and its Effect upon Commerce. *T. B. Moxon.*
Pauperism, Past and Present. *Dr. J. M. Rhodes.*
The Future Unit of Local Government. *A. M. Lazarus-Langdon.*
The Taxation of Land Values. *Rev. H. Rylett.*

Session 1891-92

Wages and Hours of Working in the Coal Industry in France, Germany, and England. *Prof. Munro.*

Bank Reserves, the Central Stock of Gold, and One Pound Notes. *G. H. Pownall.*

The Companies Act, 1862, and Subsequent Acts and Suggested Amendments. *R. M. Pankhurst.*

The Financial Crises of 1866 and 1890. *J. Sutcliffe.*

Session 1892-93

The Extent of Food Imports into the United Kingdom. *S. Bourne.*

The Effect of the Taxation of Land Values on Local Rates. *Rev. H. Rylett.*

A Statistical View of some Anomalies of our Educational System. *Rev. J. H. Hollowell.*

Eastward Ho ! or some Considerations on our Responsibilities in the East. *Rev. L. C. Casartelli.*

Considerations in Relation to State Insurance of Old Age Pensions, and other Benefits. *E. Sowerbutts.*

Session 1893-94

Strikes and Economic Fallacies. *W. Fogg.*

The Objective Causes of Pauperism. *Dr. J. M. Rhodes.*

The Future of the Voluntary Schools. *E. J. Broadfield.*

The Inebriates Acts of 1879-80 in Theory and Practice, with a Suggested Amendment. *E. Neild.*

The Hours and Cost of Labour in the Cotton Industry, at Home and Abroad. *F. Merttens.*

Session 1894-95

Betterment, Worsement, and Recoupment. *W. H. S. Watts.*

The Theory of the Yearly Market Movement. *H. Binns.*

Fifty Years' Accounts of the Bank of England. *A. W. Flux.*

Local Taxation. *E. Guthrie.*

Cotton Corners. *Col. W. W. Biggs.*

Juvenile Emigration. A Social Economy. *G. R. Kirlew.*

Session 1895-96

The Government of Manchester. *T. C. Horsfall.*

The Report of the Royal Commission on the Aged Poor. *G. Rooke.*

A Fifteen Years Record of the Stock Exchange. *T. Dreydel.*

Company Law and the Report of 1895. *Dr. Pankhurst.*

Continuation Schools. *C. H. Wyatt.*

County Councils and Education. *T. Snape.*

Session 1896-97

Some Aspects of Local Government. *G. H. Pownall.*
Open Spaces for Recreation in Manchester. *H. Philips.*
Local Rates of Mortality from Consumption. *T. A. Welton.*
Registration of Electors and Registration Laws. *J. Wigley.*
The Manchester Ship Canal. *A. W. Fletcher.*
Index Numbers and the Course of Prices as Indicated by them during the last Fifty Years. *Sir W. H. Houldsworth.*
The Manchester Sewage Problem, with Suggestions for its Solution, and Suggested Amendment of the Rivers Pollution Act. *N. Bradley.*
The Conditions of Life in Angel Meadow. *Rev. J. E. Mercer.*

Session 1897-98

The English Poor Law, with Special Reference to Progress in its Administration during the Queen's Reign. *A. McDougall.*
The Municipalities of Manchester and Hamburg. *J. R. Galloway.*
Agricultural Banks and the Evils of the Money Lending System. *R. A. Yerburgh.*
Is the Birth-rate still Falling? *R. H. Hooker.*
Tramways and their Municipalisation. *Sir Bosdin T. Leech.*
Forty Years' Industrial Change in England and Wales. *T. A. Welton.*
The 1891 Census of Occupations of Males in England and Wales, so far as Relates to the Large Towns and to the Counties after the Exclusion of such Towns. *T. A. Welton.*
Compensation for Industrial Accidents. *A. W. Flux.*
Bimetallism. *Sir W. H. Houldsworth.*

Session 1898-99

Town Beauty. *Rev. Dr. L. C. Casartelli.*
Feeble-minded Children. *Miss Mary Dendy.*
The Housing Problem. *B. F. C. Costelloe.*
Some Old Trade Records Re-examined; A Study in Price Movements during the Present Century. *Prof. A. W. Flux.*
The Organisation of Educational Effort in Manchester. *Prof. A. S. Wilkins.*
Some Statistics of Lancashire Industries. *Dr. J. Niven.*

Session 1899-1900

City Government and Local Taxation in Copenhagen. *Prof. A. W. Flux.*
Statistical Aspect of Wealth and Welfare. *C. S. Devas.*
The Medical Charities of Manchester and Salford. *F. Brocklehurst.*
Primary Education. *E. J. Broadfield.*
Is Insanity Increasing? *Dr. J. M. Rhodes.*
Employers' Liability and Compensation to Workmen in Case of Accidents. *E. J. Carlisle.*

Session 1900–01

Some Thoughts on Industrial Combination. *Prof. A. W. Flux.*
The Inebriates Act, 1898. *E. Neild.*
The Middleman in Commerce. *E. Helm.*
An Historical Sketch of Masters' Associations in the Cotton Trade. *S. J. Chapman.*
Municipal Trading. *A. Woodroofe-Fletcher.*
The Growth of Foreign Competition. *F. Merttens.*
The Growth of the Population during the Nineteenth Century. *Sir Robert Giffen.*

Session 1901–02

Public-house Licences. *Sir W. H. Houldsworth.*
The Effective Use of Charitable Loans to the Poor, without Interest. *Max Hesse.*
Present Difficulties in Connection with our Art Gallery, our Reference Library, and our Royal Infirmary. *Councillor W. T. Rothwell.*
The Metrical System. *H. E. Wollmer.*
An International Gold Coinage. *C. H. Swann.*
Education for Business and Public Life. *Prof. S. J. Chapman.*
The Distribution, Growth, and Decay of Towns, 1801–1901. *T. A. Welton.*

Session 1902–03

Notes on the Census Report (1901) for the County of Lancaster. *T. A. Welton.*
The Conditions and Consequences of Market Development in the Cotton Trade. *Prof. S. J. Chapman.*
The German Tariff Maze and Most-favoured-Nation Systems. *G. Jacoby.*
The Case for a Ministry of Health. *F. Scott.*

Session 1903–04

Productivity, Protection, and Integration of Industry. *F. Merttens.*
The History and Development of the Manchester School Board. *C. H. Wyatt.*
Some Problems of Local Government. *F. Brocklehurst.*
The Work of the British Cotton-growing Association. *J. A. Hutton.*
Value and Comparability of English and German Foreign Trade Statistics. *B. Ellinger.*
The Garden Village of the Small Holdings Association. *J. Long.*

Session 1904–05

On the Recent Migrations of English People, and on some other Questions arising in Relation to the Census of 1901. *T. A. Welton.*
The Taxation of Land Values. *L. W. Zimmerman.*

The Theory of Wages in Relation to Practice.   *Prof. S. J. Chapman.*
The Organisation of Labour as a Political Force.   *A. H. Gill.*
The Gold Reserve of the Nation.   *D. Drummond-Fraser.*

Session 1905–06

The Growth of Municipal Expenditure.   *F. Brocklehurst.*
The Rise and Decline of the Free Trade Movement.   *F. Platt-Higgins.*
Ten Years' Experience of the Manchester and Salford County Courts.
   Judge E. A. Parry.
Trade Societies in the Middle Ages.   *The Very Rev. Anselm Poock.*
Some Financial and Commercial Aspects of Trade Insolvency.   *H. L.*
   Price.

Session 1906–07

A Decade of Manchester Banking, 1896–1905.   *D. Drummond Fraser.*
Some Recent Electoral Statistics.   *J. Rooke Corbett.*
Appreciation of Municipal Assets.   *F. G. Burton.*
Manchester Municipal Public Libraries.   *W. Butterworth.*
Compensation under the Licensing Act, 1904.   *F. W. Cooper.*

Session 1907–08

Death Rates.   *Dr. J. Niven.*
The Elasticity of a Tariff.   *Hilaire Belloc.*
The Administration of Elementary Education by Great Authorities.
   A. G. C. Harvey.
The Non-Commission-Paying Life Offices.   *A. H. Booth.*
The Problem of the Feeble-minded.   *Miss Mary Dendy.*

Session 1908–09

An Analysis of our Trade with Germany.   *B. Ellinger.*
The Rating of Land Values.   *J. Rooke Corbett.*
The Importance of Afforestation and its Possibilities.   *Prof. F. E.*
   Weiss.
The Progress of Tropical Medicine.   *Sir Rubert W. Boyce.*
Depression in Trade and its Causes.   *W. T. Hesketh.*

Session 1909–10

Manchester Milk Supply.   *Prof. Sheridan Delépine.*
The Trade between the United Kingdom and the United States.
   B. Ellinger.
Home Work.   *Prof. S. J. Chapman.*
Remarks upon Chinese Commerce, Banking and Economics.   *Prof.*
   E. H. Parker.
The Administration of the Lord Mayor's Fund for the Relief of Distress
   due to Unemployment.   *C. H. Wyatt.*

Session 1910–11

The Economic Waste of the Existing (or any other) Poor Law. *Sidney Webb.*

Industrial Accidents. *H. Verney.*

A Talk about the Drama. *Miss A. E. F. Horniman.*

Recent London Experiments in the Schooling of Poor Children. *Prof. J. J. Findlay.*

The Yield of High-Class Investments, 1896 to 1910. *Prof. A. W. Flux.*

The Cost of Disease. *Dr. J. Niven.*

Session 1911–12

The Problem of the Gold Reserve. *D. Drummond Fraser.*

The Theory and Finance of Modern Armaments. *F. W. Hirst.*

The Organisation of the Casual Labour Market. *R. Williams.*

International Comparisons of Labour Conditions. *C. F. Bickerdike.*

The Adolescence of the Working Lad in Industrial Towns. *J. L. Paton.*

Session 1912–13

The Economic Value of the Ship Canal to Manchester and District. *J. S. McConechy.*

The Physique of the Modern Boy : Problems Solved, and Problems Awaiting Solution. *Dr. A. A. Mumford.*

Bank Cash Reserves. *H. Mellor.*

On the Work of the Public Trustee. *C. J. Stewart.*

Guatemala ; Travels and Experiences. *W. S. Ascoli.*

Session 1913–14

Labour Co-partnership and Labour Unrest. *T. Gregory.*

The Cause of the Fall in Consols. *G. I. Murray.*

Coal Smoke ; its Causes, Consequence, and Cures. *J. W. Graham.*

The Export of Capital and the Cost of Living. *Sir George Paish.*

Industrial Recruiting and Displacement of Labour. *Prof. S. J. Chapman.*

Session 1914–15

The Longest Price of War. *Dr. Saleeby.*

The Influence of Sunspots on Prices : Professor Jevons' Theories Explained. *W. R. Hesketh.*

The Industrial Activities of the Education Committee. *Spurley Hey.*

The Occupations of the People of England and Wales in 1911, from the Point of View of Industrial Developments. *T. A. Welton.*

An Attempt to Assess the Effect of Noise on Health. *Dr. J. Niven.*

Session 1915–16

The Position of the Doctrine of " Laissez-faire " after the War. *B. Ellinger.*

M

Personal Savings and the £1 War Bonds. *D. Drummond Fraser.*
The Value of Money. *A. F. Jack.*
The Effect of the Napoleonic War on the Cotton Trade. *G. W. Daniels.*

Session 1916–17

Economic Conditions after the War. *Prof. A. Kirkaldy.*
The Quantity Theory and Bank Reserves. *W. H. Goulty.*
State Purchase of the Liquor Trade. *R. B. Batty.*
The Case for a Guild of Shippers, with some Suggestions. *B. Ellinger.*
Education after the War. *Bishop Welldon.*

Session 1917–18

Certain Influences Affecting the National Rate of Population. *The Very Rev. Mgr. Poock.*
Substituted Female Labour in War-Time. *Mrs. A. Robinson.*
Lancashire Vital Statistics as Disclosed by the last Census. *E. B. Nathan.*
The Mercantile Marine in its Relation to the State. *Sir Norman Hill.*
The Rights and Responsibilities of Capital. *Sir Hugh Bell.*
The Cotton Trade at the Close of the Napoleonic War. *G. W. Daniels.*

Session 1918–19

Housing the People. *A. W. Shelton.*
The Future of British Railways. *D. Halliwell.*
Self-Government in Industry. *G. Middleton.*
A Problem of After-War Reconstruction—the Study of Foreign Languages. *Rt. Rev. L. C. Casartelli.*
English Poor Law. *The Very Rev. Mgr. Poock.*

Session 1919–20

Our Salmon Fisheries and their Development. *J. A. Hutton.*
Currency : Its Bearing on National Reconstruction and Imperial Development. *M. B. F. Major.*
Juvenile Organisation and After-Care Committees. *J. H. Helm.*
The Present Position of the Trust Question. *Prof. D. H. Macgregor.*
Some Observations on the Economic Aspect of the League of Nations. *P. Butlin.*

Session 1920–21

Public Expenditure and the Need for Economy. *F. W. Hirst.*
Trade Boards and Minimum Rates of Wages. *J. J. Mallon.*
International Labour Organisation. *Rt. Hon. G. N. Barnes.*
Some Aspects of Trade Fluctuations. *Sir W. H. Beveridge.*
Transport. *A. Watson.*

Session 1921-22

The Economic and Financial Outlook. *Sir George Paish.*
The Relation between Mental and Physical Efficiency at the Manchester Grammar School. *Dr. A. A. Mumford.*
Proportional Representation. *P. M. Oliver.*
Railway Statistics in Great Britain. *T. A. Kenyon.*
Women's Wages in the Cotton Trade. *Mrs. D. M. Barton.*

Session 1922-23

Transport. *Sir Henry Maybury.*
The Mechanism of Reparations. *A. E. Leaf.*
Trade Unions. *A. Hopkinson.*
Boarding School and Day School : A Comparison. *J. L. Paton.*
The Experimental Study of Epidemics. *Prof. W. C. Topley.*

Session 1923-24

Air Transport and its Future Importance to the Empire. *Major-General Sir William Sefton Brancker.*
Business Statistics. *F. Roby.*
Indian Factories in the Eighteenth Century. *Prof. George Unwin.*
The Measurement of Changes in the Cost of Living. *J. Hilton.*
The Post-War Depression in the British Cotton Industry. *Prof. G. W. Daniels.*

Session 1924-25

The Census of Production. *Prof. A. W. Flux.*
Birth Rates in Lancashire and Cheshire, 1911 and 1921. *D. Caradog Jones.*
Cotton Statistics. *Prof. J. A. Todd.*
The Distribution of Capital in England. *Prof. Henry Clay.*
Some Problems of the Return to Gold. *O. R. Hobson.*

Session 1925-26

The Early History of the Manchester Statistical Society. *T. Gregory.*
Voluntary Hospital Statistics. *L. G. Brock.*
State of the Engineering Industry. *C. Bentham.*
British Export Trade since the War. *Sir William Clark.*

Session 1926-27

The Economic Position of France in Europe. *J. R. Cahill.*
Central Bank Policy. *Prof. T. E. Gregory.*
The Comparative Position of the Lancashire Cotton Industry and Trade. *Prof. G. W. Daniels and Mr. J. Jewkes.*
The International Economic Conference. *H. B. Butler.*
Garden Cities. *Dr. N. Macfadyen.*

Session 1927–28

Lancashire's Declining Trade with China—Causes and Remedies. *B. Ellinger.*
Lessons of Railway Statistics. *R. Bell.*
Industrial Peace. *E. D. Simon.*
National Debt Policy. *O. R. Hobson.*

Session 1928–29

The Course of Employment since the War. *Prof. H. Clay.*
The Raising of the School Leaving Age. *Spurley Hey.*
Neglected Factors in Production. *A. Greenwood.*
Efforts to Rationalise the Cotton Industry of U.S.A. *A. S. Pearse.*
Problems of Retail Distribution. *F. J. Marquis.*

Session 1929–30

Cyclical Fluctuations in the Railway Industry. *C. D. Campbell.*
The Dividing Line between Individualism and Socialism. *W. W. Paine.*
Fluctuations in Savings Bank Deposits. *T. S. Ashton.*
Rationalisation. *W. L. Hichens.*
Ten Years' Development of Industrial Standards in Europe. *H. B. Butler.*

Session 1930–31

Recent Changes in the Overseas Trade of the United Kingdom. *Prof. G. W. Daniels.*
Some Problems of the Manchester Merchant after the Napoleonic Wars. *Dr. A. Redford.*
French Monetary Policy. *R. G. Hawtrey.*
The Recruitment of Juvenile Labour in Warrington. *C. Bottomley.*
The World's Oil Industry, 1920–1930. *C. A. Cooke.*

Session 1931–32

The National Electricity Scheme. *Alderman W. Walker.*
The Citizen's Purse. *Dr. W. H. Coates.*
A Statistical Study of the Economics of Large-Scale Production. *J. Jewkes.*
The Future of the Gold Standard. *Prof. T. E. Gregory.*
The Financing of Industrial Development. *Prof. H. Clay.*

Session 1932–33

Ottawa and International Trade. *H. Glyn Hughes.*
The Statistics of Broadcasting. *E. W. Liveing.*
The Economics of Road Transport, illustrated by Statistics Relating to Lancashire. *J. Stafford.*
The Relation between Unemployment, the Mobility of Labour and the Localisation of Industry. *J. Jewkes.*
Incidence of Local Rates with Particular Reference to Changes occasioned by Recent Legislation Affecting Rates and Grants. *J. Lythgoe.*

INDEX OF AUTHORS

	Abbreviated Title	*Session*
Adamson, R.	The Theory of Money.	1884–85
Adshead, J.	Juvenile Criminals.	1855–56
	Convalescent Hospital for Manchester.	1860–61
Alford, S.	Habitual Drunkards Bill.	1876–77
Arledge, J. T.	Manufacture and Health.	1889–90
Ascoli, W. S.	Guatemala.	1912–13
Ashton, T. S.	Savings Bank Deposits.	1929–30
Ashworth, H.	The Turn-out in Preston.	1836–37
Ashworth, H. & E.	Steam Engines and Water Wheels in Bolton.	1836–37
Aspland, A.	Quarantine.	1852–53
	National Mortuary Returns.	1856–57
	Mortality of the Army.	1858–59
	Life Insurance.	1859–60
	Mortuary Tables of Paris.	1860–61
	Reformatories.	1862–63
	Presidential Address.	1863–64
	American Prisons.	1864–65
	Capital Punishment.	1866–67
	Industrial Schools.	1867–68
Aspland, L.	Votes at Elections.	1869–70
Axon, W. E. A.	Proportion of Sexes.	1873–74
	Library Statistics.	1874–75
	Deaf and Dumb Statistics.	1874–75
	English Publishing Trade Statistics.	1876–77
	Sunday Opening of Libraries.	1878–79
	Theatrical Amusements.	1881–82
	Education in Salford.	1882–83
Baines, M. A. (Mrs.)	Infant Mortality.	1868–69
Baker, H.	Growth of Manchester, 1861–71.	1871–72
	Commercial Banking.	1872–73
	Commercial Accounts at the Bank of England, 1844–75.	1875–76
	Manchester Population, 1871–81.	1881–82
	Credit of Corporate Bodies.	1882–83
	Revaluation of Annuity on the National Debt.	1883–84

	Abbreviated Title	*Session*
Baker, T. B. L.	Vagrants and Tramps.	1868–69
Barclay, R.	Bimetallism.	1881–82
Barnes, G. N.	International Labour Organisation.	1920–21
Barton, Mrs. D. M.	Women's Wages in Cotton Trade.	1921–22
Beale, S.	Statistics of Birmingham.	1835–36
Bell, Hugh.	Rights and Responsibilities.	1917–18
Bell, R.	Railway Statistics.	1927–28
Bellhouse, E. T.	Baths and Washhouses.	1853–54
	On the Banda Oriental.	1857–58
	Manchester Baths and Washhouses.	1876–77
	Coffee Houses.	1879–80
	Technical Education.	1880–81
Belloc, H.	Elasticity of a Tariff.	1907–08
Bentham, C.	Engineering Industry.	1925–26
Beveridge, W.	Trade Fluctuations.	1920–21
Bickerdike, C. F.	International Labour Conditions.	1911–12
Biggs, W. W.	Cotton Corners.	1894–95
Binney, E. W.	Geology of Manchester.	1841–42
Binns, H.	The Yearly Market Movement.	1894–95
Blackley, W. L.	National Insurance.	1879–80
Booth, A. H.	Non-Commission-Paying Life Offices.	1907–08
Bottomley, C.	Juvenile Labour in Warrington.	1930–31
Bourne, S.	Food Supplies of Britain.	1876–77
	Imports and Exports.	1878–79
	Deficient Harvests and Exports.	1881–82
	Food Imports into the U.K.	1892–93
Boyce, R. W.	Tropical Medicine.	1908–09
Bradley, N.	Manchester Sewage.	1896–97
Brancker, W. S.	Air Transport.	1923–24
Bremner, J. A.	Compulsory Education.	1869–70
	Prison Discipline.	1873–74
Broadfield, E. J.	Education Act, 1870.	1888–89
	Voluntary Schools.	1893–94
	Primary Education.	1899–90
Brock, L. G.	Voluntary Hospital Statistics.	1925–26
Brocklehurst, F.	Manchester Medical Charities.	1899–00
	Local Government.	1903–04
	Municipal Expenditure.	1905–06
Broderick, L.	Proportional Representation.	1884–85
Browning, T.	Middle Class Education.	1861–62
	Alleged Depreciation of Gold.	1864–65
Burton, F. G.	Municipal Assets.	1906–07
Butler, H. B.	International Economic Conference.	1926–27
	Development of Industrial Standards.	1929–30
Butlin, P.	Economic Aspect of the League of Nations.	1919–20

	Abbreviated Title	*Session*
Cahill, J. R.	Economic Position of France.	1926–27
Callender, W. H.	Provision of Education.	1852–53
	The Crisis of 1857.	1857–58
Campbell, C. D.	Cyclical Fluctuations in Railways.	1929–30
Carlisle, E. J.	Employers' Liability.	1899–00
Casartelli, L. C.	Commercial Education.	1881–82
	Teaching of Modern Languages.	1887–88
	Responsibilities in the East.	1892–93
	Town Beauty.	1898–99
	Study of Foreign Languages.	1918–19
Chadwick, D.	The Recording of Vital Statistics.	1860–61
	Education and Conditions: Manchester and Salford.	1861–62
Chadwick, E.	Labourers on Railways.	1845–46
Chapman, S. J.	Masters' Associations.	1900–01
	Business Education.	1901–02
	Market Development in Cotton Trade.	1902–03
	Theory of Wages.	1904–05
	Home Work.	1909–10
Chapman, S. J., and Shimmin, A. N.	Displacement of Labour.	1913–14
Cherry, A. H.	Economic Aspects of Banking.	1888–89
Chorlton, T.	Poor Law.	1875–76
Christie, R. C.	Economic Views of Greek Philosophers.	1856–57
Clark, W.	British Post-War Trade.	1925–26
Clay, H.	Distribution of Capital in England.	1924–25
	Post-War Employment.	1928–29
	Financing of Industrial Development.	1931–32
Coates, W. H.	The Citizen's Purse.	1931–32
Condor, F. R.	Conveyance between Manchester and Liverpool.	1882–83
Cooper, F. W.	Compensation under the Licensing Act, 1904.	1906–07
Corbett, J. R.	Election Statistics.	1906–07
	Land Values.	1908–09
Costelloe, B. F. C.	Housing.	1898–99
Credland, W. R.	Free Libraries in Manchester.	1887–88
Crompton, S.	Mortality from Burns and Scalds.	1849–50
	Prevention of Small-pox.	1858–59
Daniels, G. W.	Effect of the Napoleonic War on the Cotton Trade.	1915–16
	Cotton Trade at the Close of the Napoleonic War.	1917–18
	Post-War Cotton Trade Depression.	1923–24
	Changes in U.K. Overseas Trade.	1930–31

	Abbreviated Title	*Session*
Daniels, G. W., and		
Jewkes, J.	Lancashire and World Cotton.	1926–27
Darbishire, S. D.	Court of Requests and the Court Baron.	1834–35
Delépine, S.	Manchester Milk Supply.	1909–10
Dendy, Mary	Feeble-minded Children	1898–99
	Feeble-minded.	1907–08
Devas, C. S.	Wealth and Welfare.	1899–00
Dickins, T.	Social Condition of the Poorer Classes.	1864–65
	Treatment of Prisoners.	1875–76
	Social Condition of the Time.	1877–78
	Border-Land of Pauperism.	1879–80
	Juvenile Offenders.	1880–81
Dickinson, W. L.	Hulme's Educational Charity.	1868–69
Dreydel, T.	Stock Exchange.	1895–96
Dunn, James.	Emigration, its Effects on Commerce.	1853–54
Duppa, M.	Conditions in Marylebone and Kent.	1836–37
Ellinger, B.	English and German Foreign Trade Statistics.	1903–04
	Analysis of our Trade with Germany.	1908–09
	Trade between U.K. and U.S.A.	1909–10
	Laissez-faire after the War.	1915–16
	A Guild of Shippers.	1917–18
	Lancashire's Declining Trade with China.	1927–28
Elliott, T. H.	Taxation and Rating.	1887–88
Fielden, J. C.	Surplus Labour in Periods of Depression.	1881–82
Fielding, Rev. H.	Felons in Salford.	1834–35
Findlay, J. J.	Schooling Poor Children.	1910–15
Fitzgerald, M.	Union with Ireland.	1859–60
Fletcher, A. W.	The Manchester Ship Canal.	1896–97
	Municipal Trading.	1900–01
Flux, A. W.	Accounts of the Bank of England.	1894–95
	Compensation for Industrial Accidents.	1897–98
	Old Trade Records.	1898–99
	City Government in Copenhagen.	1899–00
	Industrial Combination.	1900–01
	Yield of High-Class Investments.	1910–11
	Census of Production.	1924–25
Fogg, W.	Free Trade.	1886–87
	Strikes and Economic Fallacies.	1893–94
Fraser, D. D.	Gold Reserve.	1904–05
	Manchester Banking, 1896–97.	1906–07
	Gold Reserve.	1911–12
	£1 War Bonds.	1915–16

	Abbreviated Title	*Session*
Galloway, J. R.	Social Conditions.	1889–90
	Manchester and Hamburg.	1897–98
Gibson, R. H.	England in the Fourteenth and Fifteenth Centuries.	1870–71
	Population, Sixteenth and Nineteenth Centuries.	1875–76
	Statistics of New Zealand.	1883–84
	Statistics of New Zealand.	1889–90
Gibson, W. W.	Ardwick Sick and Burial Society.	1836–37
Giffen, R.	Growth of Foreign Competition	1900–01
Gifford,	Vagrants : Mode of Life.	1851–52
Gill, A. H.	Labour as a Political Force.	1904–05
Goodier, J.	Municipal Finance.	1877–78
Goulty, W. H.	Quantity Theory and Bank Reserves.	1916–17
Graham, J. W.	Coal Smoke.	1913–14
Graham, W.	Socialism.	1887–88
Greaves, G.	Homes for Working Classes.	1860–61
	Causes of Infanticide.	1862–63
	Law Relating to Abortion.	1863–64
	Sewer Rivers.	1865–66
Greenwood, A.	Neglected Factors in Production.	1928–29
Greg, S.	Present State of Education.	1833–34
	Medical Statistics.	1837–38
	Criminal Statistics.	1837–38
	Education in Macclesfield.	1838–39
Greg, S. & W. R.	Condition of Manchester Cotton Operatives.	1833–34
Greg, W. R.	Criminal Statistics.	1833–34
	Number of Churches and Population.	1834–35
	Report of Factory Inspectors.	1834–35
	Consumption of Coal : London, 1833–34 ; Manchester, 1833.	1835–36
	National Education.	1837–38
	Statistical Desiderata.	1837–38
	Rate of Mortality.	1841–42
Gregory, T.	Labour Co-partnership.	1913–14
	Early History of the Society.	1925–26
Gregory, T. E.	Central Bank Policy.	1926–27
	Future of the Gold Standard.	1931–32
Guthrie, E.	The Decimal System.	1880–81
	Effect of " Cornering."	1881–82
	Socialism and Individualism.	1885–86
	Presidential Address.	1888–89
	Local Government.	1889–90
	Local Taxation.	1894–95
Hald, E., and M. Kreiberg.	Education in Denmark.	1856–57

	Abbreviated Title	*Session*
Hale, E. J.	Constitution of the U.S.A.	1887–88
Halliwell, D.	British Railways.	1918–19
Hamlin, M. (Mrs.)	Property at Sea in War.	1868–69
Hampson, J. W.	Local Authorities and Central Boards.	1858–59
Hannam, W. T.	Principle of Assurance.	1858–59
	Life Assurance and Investment.	1859–60
	Bonus Systems of Life Assurance.	1861–62
Harrison, G. M.	Relief during Present Distress.	1862–63
Harvey, A. G. C.	Elementary Education.	1907–08
Hawtrey, R. G.	French Monetary Policy.	1930–31
Helm, E.	Cotton Trade, 1862–68.	1868–69
	Trades Unions.	1870–71
	American Crisis, 1873.	1873–74
	Silver.	1877–78
	Trade Depression.	1878–79
	Trade Revival.	1879–80
	The Middleman in Commerce.	1900–01
Helm, J. H.	Juvenile After-Care Committees.	1919–20
Herford, C. J.	Slavery in America.	1861–62
	Boarding and Training Pauper Orphans.	1872–73
Herford, E.	Treatment of Juvenile Offenders.	1841–42
	Fallacies of Political Economy.	1853–54
	The Science of Wealth.	1860–61
	Important Economic Problems.	1861–62
	Municipal Institutions.	1864–65
	Currency and Finance.	1867–68
	Facts and Fictions of Currency.	1874–75
	Coroners.	1876–77
Hesketh, W. T.	Trade Depression.	1908–09
	Influence of Sunspots on Prices.	1914–15
Hesse, Max.	Loans to the Poor.	1901–02
Hewitt, T.	Registration of Titles to Land.	1880–81
Hey, Spurley.	Education Committees.	1914–15
	Raising of School Leaving Age.	1928–29
Heywood, B.	Conditions in Irlams-o'-th'-Height.	1834–35
	The Promotion of Literature in Manchester.	1834–35
Heywood, J.	Conditions in Miles Platting.	1837–38
	Conditions in Westminster.	1839–40
	Schools in Larne, Ireland.	1840–41
	Trinity College, Cambridge.	1840–41
	University Education.	1852–53
	University of Oxford.	1854–55
	Cambridge Academical Statistics.	1855–56
Hichens, W. L.	Rationalisation.	1929–30
Higgins, F. P.	Free Trade Movement.	1905–06

	Abbreviated Title	*Session*
Hildebrandt, A.	Coroners' Juries.	1876–77
Hill, Norman.	Mercantile Marine.	1917–18
Hilton, J.	Cost of Living.	1923–24
Hincks, Sir F.	Currency and Banking.	1875–76
Hirst, F. W.	Armaments.	1911–12
	Public Expenditure and Economy.	1920–21
Hobson, O. R.	Return to Gold.	1924–25
	National Debt Policy.	1927–28
Holland, P. H.	Causes of Death.	1842–43
Hollowell, J. H.	Anomalies of Educational System.	1892–93
Hooker, R. H.	Birth Rate.	1897–98
Hooley, W.	Bullion Reserve in the Bank of England.	1859–60
Hopkinson, A.	Trade Unions.	1922–23
Horniman, A. E. F.	Drama.	1910–11
Horsfall, T. C.	Government of Manchester.	1895–96
Houldsworth, W. H.	Colonisation.	1888–89
	Price Index Numbers.	1896–97
	Bimetallism.	1897–98
	Public-house Licences.	1901–02
Hoyle, W.	The Waste of Wealth.	1871–72
	The United Kingdom Alliance.	1875–76
	Conditions of Good Trade.	1879–80
Hughes, H. G.	Ottawa and International Trade.	1932–33
Hughes, W.	Elementary Education in Manchester.	1875–76
Hutton, J. A.	British Cotton-growing Association.	1903–04
	Salmon Fisheries.	1919–20
Hyde, J.	Diseases of Cattle and Price of Meat.	1877–78
Illingworth, T.	Distribution of Wealth.	1885–86
Jack, F.	Value of Money.	1915–16
Jacoby, G.	German Tariff and M.F.N. Clause.	1902–03
James, P. M.	Aborigines in British Colonies.	1837–38
Jevons, W. S.	Control of Post Office Telegraphs.	1866–67
	International Monetary Convention.	1867–68
	Work of the Society.	1868–70
	Theory of Political Economy.	1874–75
	United Kingdom Alliance.	1875–76
	Autumnal Pressure in the Money Market.	1875–76
Jewkes, J.	Large-Scale Production.	1931–32
	Unemployment.	1932–33
Jewkes, J., and Daniels, G. W.	Lancashire and Cotton Industry.	1926–27
Jones, D. C.	Birth Rate of Lancashire and Cheshire, 1911 and 1921.	1924–25
Jones, H. L.	Plan for University in Manchester.	1835–36

	Abbreviated Title	*Session*
Jones, H. L.	Consumption of Food in Lyons.	1838–39
	Savings Banks in France.	1838–39
	Education in France.	1841–42
	Trade and Commerce in France.	1841–42
Kay, Alex.	Educational Charity Founded by William Hulme.	1854–55
Kay, J.	Children in English and German Towns.	1852–53
Kay, J. P.	Objects of the Society.	1833–34
	Constitution of Dispensaries.	1833–34
	Miners in Derbyshire.	1833–34
	Public Swimming-Baths.	1833–34
	Religious Instruction of the Working Classes.	1834–35
Kenyon, T. A.	British Railways.	1921–22
Kirkaldy, A.	Conditions after the War in Great Britain.	1916–17
Kirlew, G. R.	Facts Relating to Street Children.	1888–89
	Juvenile Emigration.	1894–95
Kreiberg and Hald.	Education in Denmark.	1856–57
Lamport, C.	Amount of Railway Investment.	1847–48
	Agricultural Statistics.	1847–48
Langdon, A. M. L.	Future Unit of Local Government.	1890–91
Langley, E.	Silver.	1878–79
Langton, W.	Population of Manchester, 1831.	1833–34
	Churches, etc., in Manchester and District.	1834–35
	Employment in Ancoats.	1836–37
	Steam and Water Power in Manchester.	1836–37
	Handloom Weavers in Miles Platting.	1838–39
	Abuses of Medical Charities.	1839–40
	Religious Denominations in Hull.	1839–40
	Conditions of Working Classes in Hull.	1840–41
	Records of the Collegiate Church since 1575.	1841–42
	Commercial Accounts of the Bank of England.	1857–58
	The Work of the Society.	1867–68
	Review of a Paper by E. Herford.	1868–69
	Savings Banks.	1877–78
	Savings Bank Legislation.	1880–81
Leaf, A. E.	Reparations.	1922–23
Leech, B. T.	Municipal Tramways.	1897–98
Leggett, R. A.	Prisons and the Prison Bill.	1877–78

	Abbreviated Title	*Session*
Levi, L.	Morals in the last Twenty-five Years.	1883–84
Lewis, W. D.	Popular Errors concerning Law.	1857–58
Little, G. H.	The Court of Bankruptcy.	1858–59
	The Future of India.	1859–60
Liveing, E. W.	Statistics of Broadcasting.	1932–33
Loch, G.	Brussels and Antwerp Railway.	1836–37
Long, J.	Garden Village and Small Holdings.	1903–04
Lythgoe, J.	Incidence of Local Rates.	1932–33
Macfadyen, N.	Garden Cities.	1926–27
Macgregor, D. H.	Trusts.	1919–20
Machaffie, D.	Working Men's Comforts.	1863–64
Macleod, H. D.	Science of Economics.	1886–87
McConechy, J. S.	Manchester Ship Canal.	1912–13
McConnel, W.	Consumption of Meat in Manchester.	1837–38
McDougall, A.	English Poor Law.	1897–98
	Municipalities of Manchester and Hamburg.	1897–98
Major, M. B. F.	Currency.	1919–20
Mallon, J. J.	Trade Boards.	1920–21
Marquis, F. J.	Problems of Retail Distribution.	1928–29
Martin, R.	Intemperance and Disease.	1873–74
	Sanitary Progress in Manchester.	1874–75
Maybury, H.	Transport.	1922–23
Mayson, J. S.	Malays of Cape Town.	1854–55
Meadows, J.	Coal brought into Manchester in 1834.	1837–38
Medcalf, W.	Effect of Australian Discoveries.	1852–53
	Municipal Institutions of Manchester.	1853–54
	Municipal Government.	1855–56
	Crime in England.	1857–58
	Miners in the Erewash Valley.	1863–64
Mellor, H.	Bank Cash Reserve.	1912–13
Mercer, J. E.	Angel Meadow, Manchester.	1896–97
Merttens, F.	Hours and Cost of Labour in Cotton.	1893–94
	Growth of Foreign Competition.	1900–01
	Productivity, Protection, and Integration of Industry.	1903–04
Middleton, G.	Self-Government in Industry.	1918–19
Mills, H. V.	Home Colonisation.	1889–90
Mills, J.	Credit Cycles and Commercial Crises.	1867–68
	Post-Panic Period, 1866–70.	1870–71
	Statistical Method.	1871–72
Montgomery, R.	Bank of England Reserve in the last Ten Years.	1874–75
	Silver.	1879–80
	Remedy for Scarcity of Gold.	1882–83
	Manchester : 1834 and 1884.	1884–85

	Abbreviated Title	*Session*
Morrell, J. C.	Pollution of Rivers.	1874–75
Moxon, T. B.	Variations in Rate of Discount.	1877–78
	Indian Finance.	1880–81
	National Income and Expenditure.	1883–84
	Basis of Social Prosperity.	1886–87
	Bank Note System.	1890–91
Mumford, A. A.	Physique of Modern Boy.	1912–13
	Mental and Physical Efficiency in Manchester Grammar School.	1921–22
Munro, A.	Unemployed Females.	1862–63
Munro, J. E. C.	Sliding Scales in the Iron Industry.	1885–86
	Wages and Hours in the Coal Industry.	1891–92
Murray, G. I.	Fall in Consols.	1913–14
Nathan, E. B.	Vital Statistics of Lancashire.	1917–18
Neale, E. V.	Social Aspects of Co-operation.	1886–87
Neild, E.	Inebriates Acts, 1879–80.	1893–94
	Inebriates Act, 1898.	1900–01
Niven, J.	Lancashire Industry.	1898–99
	Death Rate.	1907–08
	Cost of Disease.	1910–11
	Effect of Noise on Health.	1914–15
Noble, D.	Medical Relief for the Sick Poor.	1849–50
	Poor Law Medical Relief System.	1855–56
	Coroners' Courts.	1858–59
	Fallacies Concerning Epidemic Disease.	1859–60
	Fluctuations in the Death Rate.	1863–64
	Value of Statistics.	1865–66
Nuttall, W.	Landowners of England and Wales.	1875–76
Oats, H. C.	Educational Conditions in Deansgate.	1864–65
	Educational Conditions in Ancoats.	1865–66
	Social Statistics of Lancashire and Cheshire.	1866–67
O'Connor, W. A.	Poor Law.	1880–81
	Land Laws.	1882–83
	Aspect of Wealth Distribution.	1885–86
Ogden, J.	The Growth of Cotton.	1863–64
O'Hanlon, W.	Medical Charities.	1872–73
Oliver, P. M.	Proportional Representation.	1921–22
Ollerenshaw, J. C.	Export of Cotton Goods to India.	1869–70
Page, F. H.	Civil Aviation.	1930–31
Paine, W. W.	Individualism and Socialism.	1929–30
Paish, G.	Exports of Capital and Cost of Living.	1913–14
	Economic and Financial Outlook.	1921–22
Palgrave, R. H. I.	Note Circulation.	1876–77

	Abbreviated Title	*Session*
Pankhurst, R. M.	Local Courts of Commerce.	1865–66
	Private Property at Sea.	1868–69
	Land and the Nation.	1883–84
	International Arbitration.	1887–88
	The Companies Act, 1862.	1891–92
	Company Law.	1895–96
Parker, E. H.	Chinese Commerce and Banking.	1909–10
Parry, E. A.	Manchester County Court.	1905–06
Paterson, —.	Diet of the Poor and Tenure of Landed Property.	1854–55
Paton, J. L.	Adolescence.	1911–12
	Boarding and Day Schools.	1922–23
Pearse, A. S.	Rationalisation of Cotton in U.S.A.	1928–29
Philips, H.	Open Spaces in Manchester.	1896–97
Poock, A.	Trade Societies in Middle Ages.	1905–06
	Rate of Population.	1917–18
	English Poor Law.	1918–19
Potter, T.	Jurisprudence in Relation to Commerce.	1858–59
Pownall, G. H.	Banking Statistics.	1876–77
	Capital and Labour.	1878–79
	Local Taxation and Government.	1884–85
	Bank Reserves : Gold and £1 Notes.	1891–92
	Local Government.	1896–97
Price, B.	Doctrine of Rent.	1871–72
Price, H. L.	Trade Insolvency.	1905–06
Ransome, A.	Vital Statistics of Towns.	1887–88
Rawlinson, R.	Railway Contracts and Railway Workmen.	1845–46
Redford, A.	Manchester Merchants after the Napoleonic Wars.	1930–31
Rees, W.	Audit of Public Accounts.	1865–66
Reynolds, J. H.	Technical Education.	1886–87
Rhodes, J. M.	Pauperism ; Past and Present.	1890–91
	Objective Causes of Pauperism.	1893–94
	Insanity.	1899–00
Richards, R. C.	Effect of the Position of Landlords on Commerce and Agriculture.	1887–88
Richson, C.	Fallacies in the " Returns " of the Number of Day Schools, etc., 1853.	1853–54
	Education of Pauper Children.	1854–55
	National System of Education.	1855–56
	Importance of Statistics.	1857–58
	Introduction of Decimal Coinage.	1858–59
Roberton, J.	Proportion of Male and Female Population.	1839–40
	Poverty in Manchester.	1839–40

	Abbreviated Title	*Session*
Roberton, J.	Outdoor Relief Widows.	1840–41
	Medical Statistics of Negroes.	1841–42
	Registration Committee.	1841–42
	Early Marriage in Oriental Countries.	1842–43
	Births, Deaths, Marriages.	1843–44
	Influence of Climate on Female Puberty in Greece.	1843–44
	Effect of Climate on Man.	1844–45
	Physiology of Hindoos.	1844–45
	Evils Affecting Railway Labourers.	1845–46
	Effect of Poverty in Accelerating Increase of Population.	1847–48
	Improvement of Manchester's Climate.	1849–50
	Influence of Land Tenure on Cultivation.	1851–52
	Land Laws.	1851–52
	Glasgow Refuges for Criminals.	1852–53
	Municipal Government.	1852–53
	Municipal Government in Manufacturing Towns.	1853–54
	National Schools of Ireland.	1854–55
	Construction and Ventilation of Hospitals.	1855–56
	Legalised Forms of Temptation.	1856–57
	Improvement of Hospitals.	1857–58
	Health of Cornish Miners.	1858–59
	Model Warehouse.	1859–60
	Hospital Accommodation in Manchester.	1860–61
	Ventilation of Houses.	1861–62
	Free Compulsory Education.	1864–65
Robinson, A. (Mrs.)	Female Labour in War-time.	1917–18
Robinson, G. T.	Town Dwellings for Working Classes.	1871–72
Robinson, S.	Sunday Schools in Dukinfield.	1838–39
	Education in Manchester, 1851.	1865–66
	Religious and Secular Education.	1869–70
Roby, F.	Business Statistics.	1923–24
Romilly, H.	Classification of Offences.	1834–35
Rooke, G.	English Poor Law.	1878–79
	Royal Commission on the Aged Poor.	1895–96
Roscoe, Sir H.	Technical Education.	1888–89
Rothwell, W. T.	Manchester Art Gallery, etc.	1901–02
Rumsey, H. W.	Life Tables as Evidence of Sanitary Conditions.	1866–67
	Population Statistics for Sanitary Organisation.	1869–70
	Fallacies in Local Rates of Mortality.	1871–72

	Abbreviated Title	*Session*
Rylett, H.	Taxation of Land Values.	1890–91
	Taxation of Land Values and Local Rates.	1892–93
Saleeby, C. W.	The Longest Price of War.	1914–15
Scott, F.	Benevolent Effort in Manchester.	1884–85
	Conditions and Occupations in Manchester and Salford.	1888–89
	Case for Ministry of Health.	1902–03
Service, S.	Index of Parish Registers.	1858–59
Shelton, A. W.	Housing.	1918–19
Sheppard, —.	Vagrancy Statistics for South Lancashire.	1851–52
Shuttleworth, J.	Fine Spinning Mills in Manchester, 1832.	1838–39
Simon, E. D.	Industrial Peace.	1927–28
Slagg, J.	Technical Education in England and Foreign Countries.	1883–84
Snape, T.	County Councils and Education.	1895–96
Sowerbutts, E.	State Insurance of Old Age Pensions.	1892–93
Spencer, J.	Growth of the Cotton Trade.	1876–77
Stafford, J.	Economics of Road Transport.	1932–33
Stanley, Rev. E.	Education and Religion in Alderley.	1834–35
	Statistical Report on Alderley.	1835–36
Steinthal, S. A.	Licensing Laws.	1868–69
Stewart, C. J.	The Public Trustee.	1912–13
Summers, W.	English Land Question.	1878–79
Sutcliffe, J.	Crises of 1866 and 1890.	1891–92
Swann, C H.	International Gold Standard.	1901–02
Syson, E. J.	Mortality in Large Towns.	1870–71
Taylor, Rev. J. J.	Two Schools in a Populous District of Manchester.	1839–40
Taylor, S.	Profit Sharing.	1882–83
Todd, J. A.	Cotton Statistics.	1924–25
Topley, W. C.	Epidemics.	1922–23
Torr, J. B.	Legislation and the Growth of Crime.	1862–63
Traice, W. H. J.	Adult Education.	1876–77
	A Patent Law.	1881–82
Unwin, G.	Indian Factories : Eighteenth Century.	1923–24
Verney, H.	Industrial Accidents.	1910–11
Vincent, C. E. H.	British Empire and Imperial Federation.	1886–87
Walker, R. B.	Organisation of Societies.	1870–71
	Census.	1874–75

N

	Abbreviated Title	*Session*
Walker, W.	National Electricity Scheme.	1931–32
Watkin, J. W.	Cost of Law and Justice in United Kingdom.	1858–59
	On the Union with Scotland.	1859–60
Watson, A.	Transport.	1920–21
Watson, R. S.	Arbitrations in Trade Disputes.	1889–90
Watts, J.	Co-operation.	1872–73
	First Manchester School Board.	1873–74
	Primary Education.	1878–79
	Elementary Education in Manchester.	1882–83
	School Board in Manchester.	1885–86
Watts, W. H. S.	Married Women's Property Act, 1882.	1882–83
	Administration of Justice in Lancs.	1884–85
	Betterment, Worsement, and Recoupment.	1894–95
Webb, S.	Poor Law.	1910–11
Weiss, F. E.	Afforestation.	1908–09
Weldon, J. E. C.	State Purchase of Liquor Trade.	1916–17
Welton, T. A.	Census of 1871.	1871–72
	Emigration : Proportion of Sexes.	1874–75
	Meaning of Statistics.	1874–75
	Census (two papers), 1871.	1875–76
	Stationary Populations.	1879–80
	Published Results of the Census 1881.	1881–82
	Mortality from Consumption.	1896–97
	Forty Years Industrial Change.	1897–98
	Census of Occupations.	1897–98
	Towns, 1801–1901.	1901–02
	Census of Lancashire, 1901	1902–03
	Census 1901 : Migration.	1904–05
	Occupations in England and Wales.	1914–15
Wembergue, F. E.	Popular Education in France.	1838–39
Whiley, H.	Manchester Corporation Health Dept.	1885–86
Whyte, J.	Cost of our Drinking Customs.	1889–90
Wigley, J.	Registration of Electors.	1896–97
Wilkins, A. S.	University Endowments.	1870–71
	Ancient and Modern Luxury.	1872–73
	Education in Manchester.	1898–99
Wilkinson, T. R.	Educational and other Conditions in Gaythorne and Knott Mill.	1867–68
	Infant Mortality.	1870–71
	History of the Manchester Statistical Society.	1875–76
Williams, R.	Casual Labour.	1911–12
Williams, T. H.	Money.	1850–51
	Effect of Increase in Quantity on the Value of Gold.	1852–53

	Abbreviated Title	*Session*
Williams, T. H.	Money, Credit, Panics.	1856–57
	Commercial Review of 1858.	1858–59
Wollmer, H. E.	Metrical System.	1901–02
Wood, J. R.	State of Education in York, 1826.	1836–37
	Account of the Institutions at Hofwyl.	1836–37
	Worship in York.	1837–38
Worthington, T.	Homes for the Poor.	1860–61
	Pavilion Hospital, Manchester.	1866–67
Wyatt, C. H.	Continuation Schools.	1895–96
	Manchester School Board.	1902–03
	Unemployment.	1909–10
Yerburgh, R. A.	Agricultural Banks and Money Lending.	1897–98
Zimmermann, L. W.	Taxation of Land Values.	1904–05

BOOKS TO READ

THIS MONEY BUSINESS: A Simple Account of the Institutions and Working of the Banking and Financial World.

By BARNARD ELLINGER, C.B.E. Demy 8vo. 144 pp.   **6s.**

This book, written by a Manchester merchant, describes simply and practically the organization and working of our banking and financial system, and shows how the various parts of the machine form one coherent whole. It is intended primarily for those with little or no previous knowledge of the subject, and should be helpful to young students and those members of the general public who are desirous of understanding the important bearing which international monetary problems have on our present distress.

CONTRIBUTIONS TO THE HISTORY OF STATISTICS.

By Prof. HARALD WESTERGAARD, of the University of Copenhagen. Demy 8vo. 288 pp.   **12s. 6d.**

Financial News.—" In this work Mr. Westergaard certainly does full justice to his subject, which is essentially one for the scholar rather than for the general reader. He has probed deep into the antique origins of the modern science of statistics, and has produced a masterly work which, despite its vast range, gives a balanced and connected account of the evolution and growth of the science to the end of the last century; and the results of his researches are presented in surprisingly readable form."

GOLD, UNEMPLOYMENT AND CAPITALISM: Essays and Addresses.

By T. E. GREGORY, D.Sc., Sir Ernest Cassel Professor of Economics in the University of London. Demy 8vo. 320 pp.   **12s.**

" Gold, Unemployment and Capitalism " is a selection from essays in a wide range of economic subjects written, with one exception, during the last eight years. The main divisions of the book—Gold, America, Central Banking, International Trade and Unemployment and Capitalism—show clearly the subjects with which Professor Gregory deals, and the whole collection is an interesting survey of what has been happening in the economic field during these last few difficult years, and of a distinguished economist's reaction to these events.

THE NEW SURVEY OF LONDON LIFE AND LABOUR.

Volume Six—Social Survey II.—Western Area.

Volume Seven—Poverty Maps to the above.

Buckram, **17s. 6d.** each volume.

Volume VI continues the statistical study, begun in Volume III, of conditions of poverty and well-being compared with those prevailing forty years ago. Volume III dealt with the Eastern half of the Survey Area; Volume VI deals with the Western half and with the Survey area as a whole. The volume also contains special studies of certain subjects related to poverty, namely, the London Housing Problem, Migration of Population, Jewish Life and Labour in East London, Household Economy, and Mental Deficiency. Volume VII shows by a system of street coloration the local distribution of poverty and welfare in the Western section of the Survey Area.

P. S. KING & SON, LTD.
14 Great Smith Street, Westminster